# Steven Spielberg

## Amazing Filmmaker

by Jim Hargrove

CHILDRENS PRESS ®
CHICAGO

## PICTURE ACKNOWLEDGMENTS

AP/Wide World Photos, Inc.—Frontispiece, pages 6, 38, 62 (2 photos), 63 (2 photos), 64 (2 photos), 65 (2 photos), 66 (2 photos), 67 (2 photos), 68 (2 photos), 69 (top), 70, 100
UPI/Bettmann Newsphotos—69 (bottom)
Cover illustration by Len W. Meents

### LIBRARY OF CONGRESS
Library of Congress Cataloging-in-Publication Data

Hargrove, Jim.
    Steven Spielberg : amazing filmmaker /
by Jim Hargrove.
      p.   cm.
    Includes index.
    Summary: Follows the life and career of the man who has directed four of the top ten money-making films of all time.
    ISBN 0-516-03263-1
    1. Spielberg, Steven, 1947-     —Juvenile literature.
2. Motion picture producers and directors—United States—Juvenile literature. [1. Spielberg, Steven, 1947-   . 2. Motion picture producers and directors.]
I. Title.
PN1998.3.S65H37   1988
791.45′0233′0924—dc19
[92]                                    87-13249
                                                 CIP
                                                 AC

# Table of Contents

Even before he was a teenager, Steven Spielberg was interested in filmmaking.

Chapter 1

# THE LITTLEST DIRECTOR

Two electric trains were speeding down the same track directly toward each other. Alongside the metal rails, little plastic people were posed for the coming disaster.

Holding an 8-mm movie camera to his eye, twelve-year-old Steven Spielberg recorded on film the gory details. One locomotive was speeding from the left, another was bearing down from the right. The plastic people looked on with plastic horror. Steven aimed the camera directly at the spot where the two trains would collide. The wait was short.

Kaboom! The two engines crashed head-on. Once again, Steven's living room was the site of a great Lionel train disaster. For toy trains, the Spielbergs' house in Scottsdale, Arizona, was incredibly dangerous territory. Trains collided there time and time again, always under Steven's watchful eye.

Arnold Spielberg, Steven's dad, held a dim view of the railroad disasters. He had helped his son build up the model train collection over a period of several years. Repeated head-on collisions were not the kinds of model railroading he apparently had in mind.

"If you break your trains one more time," the father once

warned his young son, "I'll take them away."[1] The threat gave Steven the idea to film a crash, at first using his father's camera.

Years later, after he had become a famous movie director, Steven Spielberg still cannot forget his satisfaction when he got his film back from the processor. "Then I could look at my 8-mm film over and over," he wrote, "and enjoy the demolition of my trains without the threat of losing them."[2]

Despite his father's warning, the young filmmaker was so impressed by the results of his first experiment that he continued filming other toy train wrecks, soon with his own inexpensive Kodak movie camera. "I would stage these very complex accidents on the rails," he remembered, "and, somehow intuitively, I would film these perfect crashes. When I got the film back, I would be amazed at how my little trains looked like multi-ton locomotives."[3]

Steven began devoting much of his energy and most of his free time to the making of films. Working alone in his room, he spent hours writing scripts and drawing rough pictures of camera shots on sheets of paper. Even in school, he found it difficult to concentrate. During classes, he often drew little pictures in the corners of textbook pages, flipping the pages rapidly to watch simple animation.

When he joined the Boy Scouts, his objective soon became a merit badge in moviemaking. When his father bought him a Super-8 movie camera, which has a slightly larger film image than standard 8-mm, Steven was hopelessly hooked on making movies. Already, he knew that he wanted to become a professional motion picture director.

Leah Spielberg, Steven's energetic, blond-haired and wonderfully humorous mother, looked back on how life in her household changed when her son became fascinated with the making of movies. "From then on," she said, "the decor in our house consisted of white walls, blue carpeting and tripods. My car back then was a 1950 Army-surplus jeep," she continued. "We would load it up and drive into the desert. Steven had the whole family dressed up in ridiculous costumes. He'd say, 'Stand behind that cactus,' and I actually did it. I also supplied the cold cuts."[4]

Inside his home, in the yard, and even at distant locations, the young director made his movies. He pleaded with his family—mother, father, and three younger sisters—to help him with many of his projects. Although they couldn't have realized how important their assistance was at the time, Arnold and Leah helped their young son enormously with his projects. Arnold helped Steven make miniature movie sets inside the house, using toy trucks and mountains made from paper and paste.

Somehow, Steven talked his mother into cooking thirty cans of cherries in a pressure cooker until the whole thing exploded, just so he could photograph the slimy mess all over the kitchen. "For years after that," Leah recalled, "my routine every morning was to go downstairs, put the coffee on and wipe cherries off the cabinets."[5] Although the Spielbergs lived very comfortably in a suburban setting, they were not rich. Steven's rapidly growing hobby must have been increasingly expensive. Nevertheless, his parents were astonishingly helpful and patient with their young moviemaker.

"Our living room was strewn with cables and floodlights—that's where Steven did his filming," Leah recalled. "We never said no. We never had a chance to say no. Steven didn't understand that word."[6]

But Steven was already beginning to understand the business side of motion pictures. Before long he was showing his movies to friends, making popcorn and charging admission for each screening. By his first years in high school, he was well on his way to becoming a skilled motion picture craftsman. With so much help from his family, the path was easy enough to follow. But growing up was another problem. There he encountered as many problems, and maybe more, than the average youngster.

Leah Posner, the woman who became Steven Spielberg's mother, grew up in an Orthodox Jewish home in Cincinnati and was trained as a concert pianist. She gave up pursuing a professional career when she married Arnold Spielberg, Steven's father. Arnold was an electrical engineer who worked with other people to develop some of the world's first electronic computers during the late 1940s and early 1950s. Steven once noted that his father "spoke two languages, English and computer."[7]

Near the end of 1947, Arnold and Leah Spielberg's first child, Steven, was born on December 18 in Cincinnati. For Jews as well as Christians, late December is a festive time. The eight-day Festival of Lights, or Hanukkah, a highlight of the Jewish calendar, begins around then. For Arnold and Leah Spielberg, the Hanukkah season in 1947 was a particularly blessed time.

While Arnold worked with electronic projects and early computers, Leah stayed at home to care for her young son, sometimes playing the piano with other musicians who visited her. She soon found that even a blessing could be trying at times. "Steven wasn't exactly cuddly," she recalled. "He was scary. When Steven woke up from a nap, I shook."[8]

Because Arnold's work with early computers required him to move frequently, the growing Spielberg family lived in a series of different homes when Steven was growing up. Over a period of thirteen years they moved from Cincinnati to Haddonfield, New Jersey, to Scottsdale, Arizona, and to a suburb of San Jose, California. "Just as I'd become accustomed to a school and a teacher and a best friend," Steven wrote years later, "the FOR SALE sign would dig into the front lawn and we'd be packing and off to some other state."[9]

When Steven was between the ages of nine and sixteen, his family lived in Scottsdale, and he has always regarded that Arizona city as his home.

But long before his family moved to Arizona, young Steven Spielberg already had plenty of things on his mind. One of the more significant matters involved the whole communities of monsters that he believed lived in his closet and under his bed. They were probably waiting for just the right moment to drag him off to some unspeakable fate.

Another serious matter was the crack in his bedroom wall. Exactly who, or what, lived inside it? At times he believed that a group of friendly little people lived there. At other times, he feared that ghosts would come spilling out of the crack. Once, when he had been staring at it for some time, he saw the crack actually grow much larger (probably due to the house settling a bit) as little pieces of building material fell out of it. The event must have been alarming, but there were still more things to worry about.

When Steven watched a television documentary about snakes, he cried for hours afterward. *Dragnet*, an old television show about Los Angeles policemen, also frightened him. When he was six years old, his parents took him to see Disney's *Snow White and the Seven Dwarfs*. A scene in the feature-length cartoon scared him so badly that he had to crawl in bed with his parents for several nights afterward.

The list of things that frightened him as a youngster

seems almost endless. "I was afraid of clouds, the wind, trees," the adult Steven Spielberg recalled about his childhood. "There was a forest outside my window in New Jersey, and at night the trees had silhouettes of arms and heads and tentacles. I liked being scared. It was very stimulating."[10]

As he grew a little bit older, Steven decided not to keep the thrill of being frightened just to himself. In later years, through famous movies such as *Jaws* and *Poltergeist*, he would share with the world his thrill at being scared. But when he was still a child, he enjoyed sharing his love of fear with those closest to him—especially his three kid sisters.

"When he was babysitting for us he'd resort to creative torture," Steven's sister Sue recalls. "One time he came into the bedroom with his face wrapped in toilet paper like a mummy. He peeled off the paper layer by layer and threw it at us. He was a delight, but a terror. And we kept coming back for more."[11]

Steven's youngest sister, Nancy, remembered another incident. "We were sitting with our dolls, and Steven was singing as if he was on the radio. Then he interrupted himself 'to bring us an important message.' He announced that a tornado was coming, then flipped us over his head to safety. If we looked at him, he said, we'd turn to stone."[12]

Steven himself remembers the time his sisters watched a television movie in which a Martian kept a severed head inside a fishbowl. "It scared them so much they couldn't watch it," he said. "So I locked them in a closet with a fishbowl. I can still hear the terror breaking in their voices."[13]

Nearly every member of the Spielberg family remembers some time when Steven tried to frighten his younger sisters. "He used to stand outside their windows at night," Leah Spielberg said, "howling, 'I am the moon! I am the moon!' They're still scared of the moon. And he cut off the head of his sister Nancy's doll and served it to her on a bed of lettuce."[14]

Most of Steven's early experiments with terror were directed at his sisters, but he also managed, unintentionally, to frighten his mother as well. Some of the great scares in Mrs. Spielberg's life came on those rare occasions when she dared to open the closed door leading into Steven's room. The mess was so bad that "you could grow mushrooms on the floor," she claimed. "Once his lizard got out of its cage, and we found it—living—three years later. He had a parakeet he refused to keep in a cage at all. It was disgusting. Once a week, I would stick my head into his room, grab his dirty laundry, and slam the door."[15]

Steven pretty much admits that his mother got an accurate, if brief, view of his room. "My bedroom was like all the rooms of all the kids in all the movies I've been part of," he wrote. "It was a compost heap of everything I never put away. It's still that way today. Gravity undresses me; gravity decides where my things wind up. I don't think I've used a hanger in my entire life. I've always enjoyed living in my own debris. These days, I can really mess a place up in about twelve hours. When I was a kid, I was a little bit faster: it took about 30 minutes."[16]

In his own home, Steven Spielberg was king, the older brother of three sisters and usually the center of his family's attention. But school was another matter entirely. There, he admits even today, he felt like a "nerd." A relatively small boy with glasses, acne, and skinny wrists and arms, he was often a target for the school bullies. Far from a good athlete, he was never able to do a chin-up during all the years he attended various public schools.

Steven was so unathletic at school that some of the other students, especially the athletes, called him "the retard." When sides were chosen for baseball games, he always was picked last. Once when he was in the boys' bathroom, another student threw a lighted cherry bomb at him. He barely escaped injury. Every time he got a drink of water, he was in danger of having his face pushed into the fountain by one of the larger boys. When his junior high class had the assignment to dissect a frog, he had to run outside to vomit. When he played football in gym, he often ended up with a bloody nose.

He usually ran home from school to escape attacks by other kids, not always successfully. When the journey was over, he raced into his house and straight to his room, where he slammed the door shut and shouted "Safe!" There, away from the dangers of school, where even math class was a difficult challenge, he could dream of his movies.

While he was in junior high school, motion pictures were becoming an answer to some of his problems. One of the school bullies had been making his life miserable for a year. The boy was constantly knocking Steven down, pushing his face into the dirt or the water fountain, and giving him bloody noses. Finally, Steven thought of a plan.

"I'm making this movie about fighting the Nazis and I want you to play this war hero,"[17] Steven told the bully. Although the larger boy at first made fun of the suggestion, later he agreed to play the part. In his first truly inspired casting effort, Steven made the bully the squad leader, outfitting him in a combat uniform, helmet, and backpack. The movie was called *Battle Squad*, and it must have impressed the young bully-turned-actor. Soon, he became Steven's best friend. It must have occurred to the thirteen-year-old Steven Spielberg that the movies were just what he needed.

# Chapter 2

# ON TO CALIFORNIA

Steven Spielberg attended Arizona's Arcadia High School during the early 1960s. John F. Kennedy was the president of the United States. Russian and American astronauts became the first people to orbit the earth in spaceships. A rock and roll musical group called the Beatles began to attract millions of fans, first in England and later in the United States and much of the rest of the world.

In high school, Steven was as mediocre a student as he had been in the lower grades. His parents insisted that he keep his marks high enough to pass each year, and he did, but mostly just so he could continue making movies. Some of his toughest academic struggles were in mathematics class. Only his father's frequent help enabled him to pass. In later life, his body strengthened enough to allow him, at last, to do chin-ups. But he admits that, to this day, he cannot do many arithmetic problems with fractions.

The one bright spot in Steven's high school career was Arcadia's theater arts program. "That's when I realized," he said, "there were options besides being a jock or a wimp."[1]

Another option, of course, was simply to avoid going to school. Mondays were particularly tempting. In his younger years, Steven spent his Saturdays watching old movies in a nearby theater. "They showed two feature films and a serial right in between with ten cartoons," he remembered. "It was a great Saturday. I was in the movies all day long, every Saturday."[2] By his early years in high school, he was at least as interested in making movies as in watching them.

On Mondays, the film he shot over the weekend would be ready for viewing and editing. He could cut out the shots he didn't want from the weekend and splice everything together to make a better movie. In order to avoid going to school, he would fake having a fever by holding a thermometer up to a hot light bulb until it registered an alarming temperature. His mother was wise to the scheme, but for some reason was willing to play along. "My God, you're burning up," she would say. "You're staying home today."[3] Playing his well-practiced role, Steven would moan appropriately.

It was, of course, all for a purpose. At the expense of almost everything else, including his grades at school and a normal social life, Steven was interested in making motion pictures. As a teenaged student in Arizona, he made about fifteen fully developed movies. The first was a four-minute Western shot over a period of about eight hours on a budget of $8.50. His final film in Arizona was a two-and-a-half-hour science fiction feature that he described as "one of the five worst films ever made anywhere."[4] Amazingly, the movie turned a profit for the young filmmaker.

The most ambitious film the fifteen-year-old director had made to date was called *Firelight*. It told the story of aliens from outer space who arrived on earth in UFOs. Unlike the gentle aliens found in his later movies such as *E.T.: The Extra-Terrestrial* and *Close Encounters of the Third Kind*, the aliens in *Firelight* were hostile beings. The otherworldly creatures invaded a city on the earth, tore it apart, and reassembled it on another planet.

Steven gave one of the feature roles in *Firelight* to his youngest sister Nancy, who was about eight years old at the time. In one scene, Nancy had to reach up toward a light in the sky.

"Steven had me look directly at the sun," Nancy said more than twenty years later. "'Quit squinting!' he'd shout. 'Don't blink!' And though I might have gone blind, I did what he said because, after all, it was Steven directing."[5]

When he had finished putting all the shots and scenes together, Steven discovered that he had made a movie that was two-and-a-half-hours long, about an hour longer than the average feature film. Remarkably, arrangements were made with the operators of a Phoenix movie house to show the young filmmaker's first feature-length motion picture.

"Nobody ever said no to Steven," his mother once said. "He always gets what he wants anyway, so the name of the game is to save your strength and say yes early."[6] As always, Mrs. Spielberg supported her son's efforts at making movies. She herself put up the letters on the marquee of the Phoenix movie house announcing the premiere of *Firelight*. At the opening, the movie grossed $600, leaving a $100 profit after expenses. The event must have been a highlight in Steven's life, but it was over all too soon.

"I turned sixteen and we moved to San Jose the day after the premiere in Phoenix,"[7] Steven recalled years later. Actually, the Spielbergs moved to the little town of Saratoga, a suburb of the California city of San Jose.

The area, almost directly south of San Francisco Bay, was once known as the Valley of Heart's Delight. But in 1971, an engineer named Don Hoefler published an article in an electronics magazine in which he referred to the same area as Silicon Valley, until then an insiders' term. Silicon is an element used in the production of transistors, integrated circuits, and other solid-state devices used in computers and many other kinds of electronic equipment. The integrated circuit was developed in Silicon Valley, and a huge computer industry grew up there as well, first around the town of Palo Alto, and eventually spreading southward to San Jose. In a few more years, the world's first microcomputers would be developed in the Silicon Valley. Arnold Spielberg, Steven's father, moved there to continue his own work with computers.

But the area once known as the Valley of Heart's Delight brought anything but happiness to Steven and his family. In northern California, the differences between Arnold and Leah Spielberg began to grow more serious. Although they both loved classical music and they both adored their children, they had little else in common.

"I was about 16 when our family moved from Phoenix to Northern California," Steven wrote in 1985, "and soon after, our parents separated. They hung in there to protect us until we were old enough. But I don't think they were aware of how acutely we were aware of their unhappiness—not violence, just a pervading unhappiness you could cut with a fork or a spoon at dinner every night. For years I thought the word 'divorce' was the ugliest in the English language. Sound traveled from bedroom to bedroom, and the word came seeping through the heating ducts. My sisters and I would stay up at night, listening to our parents argue, hiding from that word. And when it traveled into our room, absolute abject panic set in. My sisters would burst into tears, and we would all hold one another. And when the separation finally came, we were no better off for having waited six years for it to occur."[8]

Steven went on to explain that his parents were wonderful, how both worked hard to protect their children even when they had little to help bring themselves together. But the pain of his parents' divorce must have been almost unbearable for the sixteen-year-old boy. Similar pain can be felt by millions of movie watchers who can feel the tragedy of separation and divorce in a number of his most famous motion pictures.

During summer vacation in 1965, Steven visited his cousins in Los Angeles. During the visit, he took a tour of the Universal Pictures studio. Universal Pictures is one of the largest and most successful motion picture and television production houses in Los Angeles. The tour he took was the kind that is given on a bus every day for tourists and other people on vacation, and it was not satisfactory for Steven.

When he saw that the bus was passing by the sound stages, large buildings where scenes from many different movies are often shot, he decided to take his own tour. During a restroom break, he hid between two sound stages until the bus loaded up with tourists and drove away. Then he wandered around the Universal lot for hours.

"I met a man who asked what I was doing, and I told him my story," Steven recollected. "Instead of calling the guards to throw me off the lot, he talked with me for about an hour. His name was Chuck Silvers, head of the editorial department. He said he'd like to see some of my little films, and so he gave me a pass to get on the lot the next day. I showed him about four of my 8-mm films. He was very impressed. Then he said, 'I don't have the authority to write you any more passes, but good luck to you.'"[9]

As his mother often noted, Steven was not the sort of person to take no for an answer. The very next day, he was back at the Universal studio, this time disguised in a business suit and carrying a briefcase. He walked straight to the front gate and waved in a friendly way to the guard, as if he did such things every day. To his great relief, the guard let him pass, as he did every day for the next three months.

"It was my father's briefcase," Steven said. "There was nothing in it but a sandwich and two candy bars. So every day that summer I went in my suit and hung out with directors and writers and editors and dubbers. I found an office that wasn't being used, and became a squatter. I went to a camera store, bought some plastic name titles and put my name in the building directory: Steven Spielberg, Room 23C."[10] Aside from adolescent actors and actresses, he was undoubtedly one of the few seventeen year olds in America with his own office in a major Hollywood studio!

Steven received an astounding informal education in filmmaking on the Universal lot, but by the end of high school it was clear that his emphasis on motion pictures demanded a high price. Because he had devoted so much of his time to making movies, his grades were not good enough to allow him to enter some of California's best colleges. Two of the schools that would not accept him were the University of California at Los Angeles (UCLA) and the nearby University of Southern California (USC). Both schools, especially USC, were fast becoming meccas for young filmmakers.

At about the same time Steven began going to college, many of today's most important moviemakers attended classes at UCLA or USC. At UCLA was Francis Ford Coppola, who later directed the *Godfather* movies and *Peggy Sue Got Married*. At USC were George Lucas (director of *American Graffiti* and *Star Wars*—and later Steven's partner in film ventures), Randal Kleiser (director of *Grease*), John Milius (director of *The Wind and the Lion* and *Conan the Barbarian*), John Carpenter (director of *Halloween*), Howard Kazanjian (producer of *Return of the Jedi*), Walter Murch (Coppola's film editor for *Apocalypse Now*), and many, many others.

With his already well-developed flair for making motion pictures, it only seemed natural for Steven to join the group of remarkable young filmmakers in Los Angeles. But his high school grades weren't good enough. Instead, he had to enter California State College at Long Beach, south of Los Angeles, which did not even have a film department. Soon enough, Steven invented his own film department for Long Beach State.

About two years after his summer spent gate-crashing the large Universal Pictures studio, Steven entered California State College at Long Beach, where he studied as an English major. When Steven began his college studies in 1967, American universities were entering a period of turmoil. America's involvement in the war in Vietnam was increasing dramatically, and many young people wanted no part of it.

Part of the protest movement that spread rapidly from college to college across the country was a tremendous increase in the number of young people who began taking illegal drugs. Steven was not one of them, but he quickly learned about the dangers of drug abuse.

Steven once told movie critic Gene Siskel that "when I was going to college at Cal State-Long Beach, I had a lot of friends experimenting with LSD and mescaline; and I was always taking them to the emergency room of the hospital for drug overdoses. And I never understood how they could ruin their lives with what I used to call a 'daylight sleep.' In the middle of the day, when you should be having fun, they were dropping tabs of acid and watching the filaments of a lightbulb. And I couldn't relate to that."[11] Throughout his life, Steven has never smoked, drunk hard liquor, or taken illegal drugs.

As a college student, Steven used his time to the maximum, but not all of it was spent on the college campus. He tried to cram all his courses into just two days at school. The other days he spent, once again, on the lot of Universal Pictures. There, he tried to get studio executives to look at the little 8-mm motion pictures he had made.

"They were embarrassed," he remembered, "when I asked them to remove their pictures from the wall so I could project my little silent movies. They said, 'If you make your films in 16-mm or, even better, 35-mm, then they'll get seen.'"[12]

As hard as it was to accept, the motion picture executives were giving the young filmmaker good advice. The 8-mm film that Steven had been using to make his movies was what almost all Americans used for little home movies before inexpensive videotape cameras began to be used in the 1980s. No legitimate professional films were made in 8-mm. The next larger size of film, 16-mm, was—and still is—used extensively in educational films for schools, and some foreign films.

Films made in Hollywood for American movie houses, however, were almost always made in 35-mm, a film size that when projected would give a much larger and brighter image than the smaller films. Some Hollywood motion pictures were even made using 70-mm film. The studio executives told Steven that, if he wanted to become a professional moviemaker, he had to produce a film in the professional 35-mm format.

Steven was now faced with the greatest challenge of his young career. In order to become a professional filmmaker, he had to produce a professional-quality film. And with no studio to help him, he had to do it on his own!

# Chapter 3

# AMBLIN' INTO HOLLYWOOD

As an English major at California State-Long Beach, Steven was already beginning to meet some of the other young filmmakers at southern California's more famous universities. In 1967, George Lucas at USC completed a feature-length student film called *THX 1138:4EB*. That same year, he screened his film at a number of different locations, including Royce Hall on the campus of UCLA.

Steven Spielberg was one of the students who watched Lucas's film at the UCLA screening. The movie, about a frightening futuristic society where behavior is largely controlled by machines and drugs, amazed young Spielberg. Although it was made by a young student on a tiny budget, *THX* can still be found on some pay television networks and on videocassettes. At the UCLA screening, Spielberg was briefly introduced to Lucas.

"He reminded me a little bit of Walt Disney's version of a mad scientist," Spielberg recalled of his first meeting with George Lucas. "I never had seen a film created by a peer that was not of this earth—*THX* created a world that did not exist before George designed it. It was hard to believe that here was somebody who knew this side of the camera as well as I thought I did."[1]

27

The overwhelming success of *THX*, including a number of important awards, must have given Steven new confidence that student filmmakers could make serious movies. Before long, Spielberg and Lucas became close friends. But even sooner, Steven was involved in making his own professional movie.

From his meetings with Hollywood film executives, Steven knew that he had to make a 35-mm film in order to attract attention in Hollywood. Although he had met a great many people involved in the motion picture business, ranging from students to powerful film executives, Steven had stopped making his own movies around the time his family moved to California. He began again about two years later, as a student at Long Beach.

For a time, he worked in the college cafeteria in order to earn the money he needed to shoot short movies with 16-mm film and a rented camera. But even the larger format was not good enough to impress the professional filmmakers in Los Angeles. All were accustomed to working with 35-mm or larger. Most had elaborate screening rooms in their homes where they could watch 35-mm films at their leisure. Few were set up to watch anything smaller. Although he made about six 16-mm films, he found it almost impossible to find an audience among Hollywood's professionals.

Steven finally decided to follow the advice of studio executives and make a 35-mm film. The first problem he encountered was the expense of working in the large film format, far greater than that for 8-mm and even 16-mm productions. Fortunately, he had a wealthy young friend named Denis Hoffman who was interested in becoming a movie producer. In the Hollywood system, producers may or may not have a good deal to do with the actual making of a motion picture. But they usually select many of the key people involved in the production and, most important, supply the money needed to make the film.

Denis Hoffman raised the $10,000 needed to make Spielberg's first film of professional quality. Both young men knew that a feature-length film would be terribly expensive. Even at the time, Hollywood producers routinely spent several million dollars on a feature—even more on some. Both men agreed that a short 35-mm film could save money but still attract attention from motion picture executives.

Steven decided to call his movie *Amblin'*, from the word "ambling," which means slow or leisurely walking. The movie tells the story of a boy and a girl who hitchhike from the desert to the Pacific Ocean. During the journey, the two young people meet, fall in love, and finally separate, all without speaking a single word of dialog.

Although *Amblin'* took only ten days to make, the production was exceptionally difficult. The film was shot in August of 1968 in Palm Desert, California. During the day, the temperature in the desert was well over 100 degrees. Everyone associated with the movie suffered terribly in the heat.

Despite the awful conditions, Steven was determined to be a successful director. As a child, with the help of his family, he had done just about everything needed to make his early motion pictures. He had served as writer, producer, cameraman, film editor, and director. But in *Amblin'*, he chose the more limited role of a writer and director. Instead of operating the camera himself, he used a cameraman named Allen Daviau (who later worked on *E.T.* and *The Color Purple*—two of Steven's greatest movies). Freed from the minute-to-minute demands of the camera, he could concentrate more on the other aspects of the film: acting, settings, lighting, camera angles, and so on.

When *Amblin'* was ready to be shown, Steven set up a large screening. So many people paid to see the twenty-two-minute film that producer Denis Hoffman earned back all the money he had invested in the project. A number of people marveled that such a lovely story could be told entirely without words.

Years later, Steven explained one of the secrets of his early success, admitting that he couldn't afford sound at the time. But despite its short length and lack of dialog, *Amblin'* did just what its young director hoped it would do. The twenty-two-minute film eventually won awards at film festivals in Atlanta and Venice. In 1970 it was released commercially and shown with the popular motion picture called *Love*

*Story*, starring Ali McGraw and Ryan O'Neal.

But even in 1968, two years before it was released commercially, *Amblin'* began to pay dividends for its young creator. A number of casting directors, people who find actors and actresses to fill roles in motion pictures and television shows, attended a screening of *Amblin'* in California. One of the actors in the short movie won a contract for a new role as a result of the screening.

Of course, Spielberg was less interested in finding casting directors than in impressing other executives in the business, people with the power to hire him as a director. That was the whole purpose of *Amblin'*, which was really meant to be an advertisement for his abilities. Although *Amblin'* was about to provide him with his first great break, Steven always held a rather low opinion of that early film. He once called it "a slick, very professional-looking film, although it had as much soul and content as a piece of driftwood."[2]

Nevertheless, *Amblin'* was professional enough to impress at least several important show business executives. One was Chuck Silvers. Silvers was head of Universal's editorial department and the man who had first listened to Spielberg when the teenager snuck away from the Universal tour in 1965. Silvers saw a screening of *Amblin'* and was impressed, both by the short movie and its young director. Silvers brought the movie to the attention of Sidney J. Sheinberg, the director of television operations for Universal. Sheinberg watched *Amblin'* and decided to call Steven.

"I said, 'You should be a director,'" Sheinberg remembered telling Spielberg over the phone. "And Steven said, 'I think so too.'"[3]

The next day, Steven attended a meeting with Sidney Sheinberg on the Universal lot. During their talk, the executive offered Spielberg a seven-year contract to direct Universal shows for television. For the twenty-year-old student, it was obviously the chance of a lifetime. But strangely enough, he hesitated.

"I was still several months shy of my twenty-first birthday," Steven remembered. "And I hadn't graduated college. But Sheinberg said, 'Do you wanna graduate college or do you wanna be a film director?' I signed the papers a week later."[4] He also remembered how quickly his college career ended. "I quit college so fast," he said, "I didn't even clean out my locker."[5]

At the age of twenty, Steven Spielberg seemed to have in his grasp everything he had dreamed about. Although he hadn't earned a college degree, he was the youngest director ever signed to a long-term Hollywood contract. But he was about to discover that the hectic schedules of professional television productions were far more demanding than his earlier amateur efforts at filmmaking.

Steven went directly from the campus of California State College at Long Beach to Studio 15 at Universal. There, he was to direct one of three stories in the first episode of a new television series called *Night Gallery*. The series was created by Rod Serling, the famous creator of the old *Twilight Zone* television show.

When he reported for work his first day, Steven was met at the door by Joan Crawford, a well-known movie star who had won the Academy Award for best actress back in 1945. Also starring in the *Night Gallery* episode with Joan Crawford was the actor Barry Sullivan.

In the story, Joan Crawford played a wealthy blind woman who forces a prominent plastic surgeon, portrayed by Barry Sullivan, to perform an experimental eye operation. The operation will restore her sight, but only for a short time. All too soon, she is told, her blindness will return. Desperate for even a few hours of sight, Joan Crawford has the operation. But during the night, when it is time to remove the bandages from her eyes, there is an electrical power failure. During the few hours that Crawford can see, she is surrounded by total darkness.

Working with such talented and experienced actors, Steven's job as director was simple enough. Rather than worry about the performances of the stars, he was free to concentrate on the technical aspects of the show. He made use of a number of unusual and sometimes startling camera techniques. A number of shots showed images reflected on glass surfaces. The technique was interesting in itself, but also focused attention on the blindness of the character portrayed by Joan Crawford.

Several television critics have pointed to the interesting effects created in that early *Night Gallery* program. Because they are constantly battling the clock, few directors of weekly television shows can afford to spend the time for such subtleties. But in almost no time at all, Steven discovered that he was faced with a personal disaster.

After watching rushes of the episode that Spielberg directed, the producer of *Night Gallery* was dissatisfied with a number of the scenes. They would have to be reshot! Joan Crawford and Barry Sullivan would have to act out portions of their roles again, this time for another director!

When Steven learned that some of his scenes were unacceptable, he was completely crushed. Such problems are hardly unusual in Hollywood productions, even for experienced professional filmmakers, much less first-time directors. But Steven apparently hadn't considered such a possibility. When he discovered that his first effort was far from a complete success, he nearly fell apart. "The pressure of that show was too much for me," he remembered. "I decided to take some time off, and Sid Sheinberg had the guts to give me a leave of absence."[6] It must have taken some courage. After all, the young director was signed to a seven-year contract and had, at least in part, messed up his first assignment.

Steven Spielberg left the Universal television production team for the better part of a year. During that time, he threw much of his energy into writing screenplays. Although he admits that writing has always been hard for him, at least the pressures were personal ones, without the responsibility of meeting the demands of many other people involved in filming television shows. While he was absent from Universal, he wrote three screenplays, one of which eventually became the basis for his first American theatrical motion picture, *The Sugarland Express*. Working by himself, day after day, the humiliation he felt after the *Night Gallery* episode gradually wore off.

"I suffocated in the freedom," he recalled about the period near the end of his absence. "I needed to work, and I came back to Universal and said, 'I'll do anything.' But no one would hire me."[7] Many people around the Universal lot knew that Spielberg had talent. But they were also a bit afraid of the young director. Many must have felt that he would try to create too many difficult and unusual scenes, shots that audiences might not like or understand. At the very least, he might delay the tight schedules necessary for weekly television shows.

Sidney Sheinberg summarized his coworkers' fears: "They thought Steven was avant-garde. So many people take bows for his success now, but at the time, they complained because he wanted to put the camera on the floor."[8] Eventually,

Steven went back to work by compromising with his fellow workers. As he put it, he agreed "to shoot six inches below the nostrils instead of from a hole in the ground."[9]

Back at work, Spielberg quickly regained the confidence he had lost on his first assignment. He directed episodes of a number of television shows. *The Psychiatrist* was followed by *Marcus Welby, M.D.* and then by *The Name of the Game*. His *Name of the Game* episode was entitled "LA2017." The unusual program depicted the city of Los Angeles in the year 2017, when the residents supposedly had to move underground because of terrible air pollution. The show attracted considerable interest among television viewers in general and TV professionals in particular. Before long, Steven directed the first episode of the highly popular *Columbo* television series, starring Peter Falk as an unusual but gifted police inspector.

Because some of the television shows that Spielberg directed lasted for an hour and even longer, he was quickly gaining experience in a show business form not unlike feature-length movies. During the year 1970, he directed his first true movie for television, called *Something Evil*. The story, about a haunted house, was not remarkable, but the excellent cast included Sandy Dennis, Darren McGavin, and Ralph Bellamy. The snappy pace director Spielberg gave the picture drew the attention of a number of television insiders.

Soon after, he began work on another television movie,

called *Duel*, that really put him on the fast track toward Hollywood fame.

Steven directs Goldie Hawn and William Atherton in a scene for *The Sugarland Express* in 1973.

# Chapter 4

# THE SPIELBERG EXPRESS

In 1971, twenty-three-year-old Steven Spielberg was on the back lot of the Universal studio. He was there for a casting call for a new television movie. A casting call usually means that a director is interviewing many actors or actresses to find one just right for a particular role. The role Spielberg was trying to fill, however, was that of a truck. He was about to begin filming a movie called *Duel*, and he wanted a scary-looking truck to be one of the stars.

The film's production manager assembled a group of about ten trucks on Universal's back lot. Steven had to choose one of them. As he examined the lineup of vehicles, the young director felt like a powerful general inspecting his troops. Finally, he chose the smallest of all the trucks, one with a front end that he felt could be made to look almost human.

Steven asked the art director to add two tanks near both doors of the cab. Many large trucks carry hydraulic tanks such as the ones he used, but they usually have only one, not two. Steven wanted two tanks so that the front end of the truck would seem to have ears. He also added dead bugs to the windshield so it would be more difficult to see the driver.

Finally, he painted the truck with a bubbly layer of motor oil and black and brown paint that eventually hardened in the sun. Steven had created a remarkably ugly truck, one that, when seen from the front, could look almost human. But its role in *Duel* was monstrous.

In the movie, a man played by the actor Dennis Weaver is driving a bright orange car on a highway during a business trip. He soon sees the strange-looking truck Spielberg had modified to look so menacing. Before long, it appears to develop a mind of its own, intent on destroying Dennis Weaver and his car. It rams the car from the back, tries to force him off the road, even pushes him onto railroad tracks in front of an oncoming train.

Just as Spielberg planned, the driver of the truck is never seen through the darkened windows. Only hands and a pair of boots, visible once when the cab door opens and the driver begins to step out, show that someone is inside the cab. The practically invisible driver causes Dennis Weaver a problem when, after a series of heart-stopping chases, he sees the truck parked in front of a restaurant. Weaver enters the cafe, hoping to find out who the driver is so that he can confront him. However, none of the men inside the restaurant pay much attention to him. Not knowing who to accuse, Weaver finally spots a man wearing a pair of boots like the ones he spotted on the otherwise unseen driver of the killer truck. He starts an argument with the man, but is apparently mistaken, and is soon kicked out of the restaurant.

After a number of other hair-raising encounters with the truck, Dennis Weaver finally makes a desperate plan to save himself. With the truck chasing him at breakneck speed, he puts his briefcase on top of the gas pedal, points his car toward a cliff, and jumps out. As his car careens over the side of the road, the truck follows it, finally landing on the ground far below and bursting into flames.

As the movie unfolds, the action proceeds at such a rapid pace that it is difficult for average viewers to understand how much careful planning went into the project. But even before the first scenes were shot, Spielberg made use of a planning technique he would use in most of his later theatrical films. That technique is called storyboarding.

When the movie is storyboarded, most or all of the important shots are drawn by an artist before the actual production with actors and film cameras begins. The storyboards give the director and camera people an idea of how each shot should look before the hectic shooting schedule begins. In the case of *Duel*, Steven created an unusual storyboard, one he could study in his motel room while the picture was being made on location.

Spielberg had an artist paint a long map showing the entire portion of the road on which the chase scenes in *Duel* were shot. Added to the map along the appropriate stretches of the highway were sentences describing each part of the chase. The map was so long that Steven was able to wrap it around the walls of his motel room. After each day's shooting was completed, he returned to his motel and measured the day's progress on the map, crossing out the descriptions of scenes that had been shot.

On some days, he would progress just a few inches, on better days a foot or two. The map helped him organize his thinking away from the hectic activity on location. It also helped him see in advance which scenes would require special attention. Steven made extensive use of storyboarding on all of his movies until *E.T.: The Extra-Terrestrial*.

Another technique Steven used to add to the excitement throughout the movie is a common trick employed in motion picture photography called undercranking. Motion pictures are really a long series of still pictures, called frames, each just slightly different from the next, presented rapidly on a screen. In most professional movies, twenty-four different still frames are shown every second. Because both the motion picture camera and the projector that shows the finished film move, or crank, through so many different frames every second, the illusion of movement is very strong.

In many of the scenes in *Duel*, Spielberg wanted it to appear as if the truck and car were driving extremely fast. It would be exceptionally dangerous, even for professional stunt men, to drive vehicles so fast on the narrow, winding highway depicted in *Duel*. But by undercranking the camera (making the film move more slowly) when an event is filmed, it is possible to give an illusion of great speed when the developed film is projected at the normal rate of twenty-four frames per second.

Time-lapse photography, where flowers can be seen opening from buds in just a few seconds, is an extreme example of undercranking. In *Duel*, director Spielberg used much more moderate undercranking to give the illusion that the vehicles were traveling faster than they really were. In many of the chase scenes, the camera cranked at twenty, sometimes eighteen, frames per second.

During the filming of a few scenes, the undercranking caused problems. When he saw the developed film for the first time, Steven realized that some of the chases took place too quickly, indicating that the camera hand undercranked more than planned. Unfortunately, the tight production schedule did not allow time for reshooting the scenes.

Despite a couple of technical problems, many people who saw *Duel* on television in 1971 were astounded. Here was a story with almost no plot at all and very little dialog. Most of the limited conversation in the movie was actually just Dennis Weaver talking to himself. Spielberg would have preferred to have done without it entirely, but a number of ABC television executives insisted on at least some dialog.

Even with the simple plot, the limited dialog, and the unexplained mystery of the killer truck, *Duel* was incredibly exciting! Scriptwriter Richard Matheson adapted the screenplay from his own short story. But it was Spielberg's dramatic directing that really made the unusual movie work so well on television.

Although the movie took less than two weeks to shoot, many people in the film business realized that it was as good as some theatrical releases. It was decided to release *Duel* in Europe as a theatrical film, one that could play in regular movie houses. The only problem was that, without the many ads shown on television, it wasn't quite long enough for a feature film. It was decided to add about fifteen minutes to make the film acceptable to European theater audiences.

During the initial filming, Steven had destroyed his unusual truck. Now he had to find another just like it, and he was given just two days to shoot the additional scenes needed for the European version. Fortunately, he was able to find a truck exactly like the one that had been driven over a cliff in the original *Duel*, except for an extra two feet of length between the cab and the trailer. He directed the new scenes with the longer truck, but observed that the additional length was very noticeable in the final European version.

*Duel* premiered in Europe in 1974, a year after Spielberg completed his third—and to date final—movie for television. That show, called *Savage*, starred Martin Landau and Barbara Bain. It premiered on television on March 31, 1973. The movie was about a reporter's investigation of a nominee for the United States Supreme Court. Steven did not want to direct the movie, but was ordered to do so by the studio. Most people agreed that, even as a movie for television, it was no better than average. The following year, however, *Duel* opened to rave reviews in Europe, eventually grossing about six million dollars at the box office.

Although Steven's seven-year contract with Universal was not due to expire until 1975, he was anxious to get away from television production long before that. He knew that work on theatrical pictures offered a number of improvements over television productions. Perhaps most important, directors were usually given more time to work on movies prepared for commercial release in motion picture houses. The extra time would allow directors to plan, shoot, and edit their pictures more carefully. In addition, movie directors, and everyone else connected with feature films, almost always enjoyed greater freedom of expression than their television counterparts. Budgets were usually larger, permitting greater freedom when selecting actors and locales, and setting up often expensive action scenes. Thoughts and words often banned from television shows could be expressed in theatrical motion pictures whenever scriptwriters, actors, and directors felt the movie was best served by them.

Even while he was working on his three television movies, Steven was trying to break into theatrical motion pictures in one form or another. He wrote a screenplay called *Ace Eli and Rodger of the Skies*, a story about pilots of early airplanes, and sent it to 20th Century-Fox, another huge movie studio in California. Although Spielberg wanted to direct the movie he had written, 20th Century-Fox producers David Brown and Richard Zanuck felt that he was not yet ready to direct a commercial motion picture.

"We liked the script," Richard Zanuck remembered, "but Spielberg wanted to direct it. We ran everything that he had done, and when I say everything, there wasn't that much. There were a couple of shorts and a few television shows. And although we bought the script, we didn't get Steven to direct it."[1]

*Ace Eli and Rodger of the Skies* was released as a motion picture in 1973. Directed by John Erman, the movie credits listed Spielberg as a scriptwriter. Of course, Steven was most interested in becoming a director of feature films. For a time, he tried to interest Universal in allowing him to direct *The Sugarland Express*, the screenplay he had written while on a leave of absence after his first *Night Gallery* episode. But executives at Universal, probably fearing weak box office performance, were unwilling to give him the go-ahead.

He finally was given the chance to direct his first commercial motion picture soon after he completed *Savage* for Universal's television division. The movie was called *White Lightning* and starred popular actor Burt Reynolds. Steven worked for about three months on the movie, looking for shooting locations and searching for other actors to work with Reynolds. But before he even began the actual filming, he decided that the project was not for him. "I didn't want to start my career as a hard hat journeyman director," Steven said. "I wanted to do something a little more personal."[2]

Steven's decision to back out of *White Lightning* must have required some courage. Since childhood, he had been dreaming of being a movie director. Now, he scorned his first opportunity to direct a feature film simply because he felt it was not right for him. Fortunately, a stroke of good luck came almost immediately.

Richard Zanuck and David Brown, the two producers who bought Steven's screenplay for *Ace Eli and Rodger of the Skies* when they were at 20th Century-Fox, decided to move on to other studios. They stayed for about a year and a half at Warners, and then were offered a generous contract by Universal, the same studio that held Steven's contract. Just before they moved to Universal, they began talking to agents and other movie professionals to see what kinds of projects were in the works that might interest their new studio.

"A week before we moved," Richard Zanuck reflected, "we met with Steven's agent. We were trying to find out what was happening, what projects were around. The agent told us: 'You guys like Steven Spielberg. Well, he's got a project at Universal called *The Sugarland Express*, but he can't get it off the ground. What he really needs is a heavyweight production team who can launch it some place.'

"We read the script," Zanuck continued, "and we instantly liked it. But we had to tell Steven's agent that there was a real problem. It looked as though we were going to form an alliance with Universal, and if the studio had already turned down the project, that could be very awkward for us."[3] Zanuck and Brown finally decided to try to get approval from Universal to produce the movie. They buried the script among a number of other screenplays, including one for *The Sting*, which became a famous movie and won the Academy Award for best picture in 1973.

In order for Steven to direct his first feature film, Zanuck and Brown had to gain the approval of Lou Wasserman, the powerful head of Universal and its parent company, MCA. At a meeting, the three men discussed Spielberg and his project. Wasserman explained that he and other Universal executives felt that the timing for *The Sugarland Express* was not right. However, the movie would not be an expensive production, and Wasserman was reluctant to turn his new producers down.

"We think Steve has a great future," Wasserman told Zanuck and Brown. "But I have to tell you we do not have any faith in the project. . . . Make the film, fellows. But you may not be playing to full theaters."[4]

Lou Wasserman was completely correct. Although the

film showed that Steven was already a talented director, it barely escaped losing money, and only earned a small profit after the rights were sold to television. Nevertheless, *The Sugarland Express* is an interesting movie, especially considering the fact that it was the first American theatrical film by a young director.

The story was written by Steven and two other screenwriters named Hal Barwood and Matt Robbins. It was based upon an actual event that made newspaper headlines in Texas in 1969.

In *The Sugarland Express*, a woman named Lou Jean, played by Goldie Hawn, helps her husband Clovis, played by William Atherton, escape from a Texas prison so that they can reclaim their baby. During the escape, Lou Jean kidnaps a Texas ranger at gunpoint and holds him hostage as she and Clovis flee in a stolen squad car. Pursued by dozens of police cars, the couple drive toward the town of Sugarland, where the baby has been placed in a foster home by the Texas welfare department. On the way, the pair become popular figures and are greeted in every town by large crowds. They even become friendly with their Texas ranger hostage. But the movie ends in tragedy when Clovis is gunned down by police in Sugarland.

When the picture was completed, executives at Universal, especially Lou Wasserman, knew that it was good enough to deserve a wide audience. But they also knew it was difficult to describe in just a few words. An ad campaign would be difficult. "They experimented endlessly," Richard Zanuck recalled about Universal's efforts to get the American public interested in the new film. "They would take whole cities and create new ad campaigns."[5] In some cities, Universal even paid movie houses to run the film, in hopes that it would catch on by word of mouth. Hollywood insiders call the practice "four-walling."

But all the efforts were largely unsuccessful. *The Sugarland Express* failed to capture the interest of the public. Even though he was faced with a financial flop, Steven Spielberg was already making plans for more movies before *The Sugarland Express* was released.

While he was working on *Sugarland*, producers Michael and Julia Phillips were overseeing filming of *The Sting* for Universal. The pair admired Steven's *Duel* immensely and considered it the best movie ever made for television. Michael, Julia, and Steven had a number of discussions about UFOs and the possibility of making a movie about them. By the time *The Sugarland Express* was completed, the three had already made a handshake agreement to develop a movie about UFOs. The agreement eventually developed into one of Spielberg's most fascinating movies: *Close Encounters of the Third Kind*.

Well before *The Sugarland Express* was even released to half-full movie houses, its young director found himself on his own kind of express. With one movie to consider with Michael and Julia Phillips, he was soon offered another. It would be his first great break, his first masterpiece, and, for a time, the most successful motion picture ever made.

**Chapter 5**

# SHARK SUMMER

In 1973, while work on *The Sugarland Express* was still being completed, Spielberg visited the offices of his friends and coworkers, producers David Brown and Richard Zanuck. On one of the men's desks, he saw the publisher's proofs for a new novel by writer Peter Benchley. The title of the work, not yet a printed book, was *Jaws*. It was about a great white shark that terrorizes a seacoast village.

Steven asked if he could have a proof, which is a copy of a typeset manuscript before it is put into pages for printing. When he read *Jaws*, he must have been impressed. So were Zanuck and Brown, who paid $175,000 to buy the movie rights to the unpublished book.

When the novel was published, it immediately became a national best-seller, earning a million dollars in prepublication sales before it even reached bookstores. The Universal producers now knew for certain that they owned the rights to a story that could make a very popular motion picture. But how would the movie be made?

In all probability, Spielberg very much wanted to be chosen to direct the movie of Benchley's popular book. He had the word "Jaws" printed in huge letters on a sweatshirt that he wore to various meetings. But Zanuck and Brown were skeptical. They wondered out loud whether the young director with a single not-yet-released American feature film to his credit was ready for such a complicated undertaking. Rather than beg for the job, Steven decided to play it very cool. "I just don't know," he reportedly told Zanuck and Brown about the project, "after all, it's only a shark story."[1]

Some months later, in early 1974, Universal sent Steven to Europe to publicize the premiere of the European edition of *Duel*. For different reasons, Zanuck and Brown were also in Europe. The three men held a series of meetings at the Hotel de Cap in the south of France. There, more details about the movie version of *Jaws* were settled. Spielberg was determined to play the role of a veteran director in great demand.

While still at the French hotel, Steven received a telephone call from his agent. The agent reported that the famous actor Paul Newman wanted Steven to direct a new movie called *Lucky Lady*.

"I marveled at the kid," Zanuck recalled about hearing Steven talk on the phone. "He had only one picture behind him, and that had not been released yet. He shared an agent with Paul Newman. And there he was, telling the agent, Freddie Fields, that he might do *Lucky Lady*, but not with Newman. He was twenty-four years old, and he turned down Paul Newman like he swatted a fly."[2] Richard Zanuck's recollection may have been a little inaccurate. Steven was probably twenty-six at the time. But he was certainly acting just like a powerful director at least twice his age.

Zanuck and Brown considered other directors, but they settled on Steven Spielberg. The next step was to get a finished screenplay. Peter Benchley, the author of the book, wrote a screenplay for the movie version of *Jaws*. Spielberg and others felt that a number of changes were needed to make the story work on the screen, especially to make the human stars more likable. Other writers, including Steven and Carl Gottlieb, worked on the final script. But even after the shooting began, Steven continued rewriting material.

At the same time the script was being worked and reworked, Spielberg and a growing staff of movie people had to make extensive plans. With art director Joe Alves, Steven looked at dozens of films about creatures and monsters that lived in the water. Many were shot in large tanks of water made to look like lakes or the ocean. The two men decided that only a real ocean would give the proper look to the movie version of *Jaws*.

Joe Alves began looking for a seaside village that would be appropriate for a location set. The technical requirements were staggering. First, a true ocean resort town, with attractive cottages and beaches, was needed. The water offshore had to be protected from wind and waves, as it is in a bay, so that camera shots would not be too shaky.

On the other hand, there had to be wide views of the open

sea to give the impression of an adventure far out in the ocean. A smooth, sandy bottom was needed twenty-five to thirty-five feet below the surface of the water, so that divers could work on underwater sequences. Tides had to be small enough to be manageable. Finally, a hotel large enough to hold a movie crew of more than one hundred people had to be within a forty-five-minute commute of the little resort town.

Despite the many technical requirements, Joe Alves discovered that a tiny village on the well-known island of Martha's Vineyard, just off the coast of Massachusetts, was ideal. There was, however, a much greater problem.

*Jaws* was, of course, a movie about a great white shark, one of the fiercest and most frightening animals in the world. Who, or what, would play the title role?

For a time, Spielberg and Alves hoped that a trained shark could be used in underwater sequences with a midget actor to make the fish look bigger. There were several problems. Steven soon discovered that there was no such thing as a trained shark.

Actor Carl Rizzo, who is four feet, one inch tall, was sent to Australia, where it was hoped he could film some test scenes with experienced shark photographers Ron and Valerie Taylor. But just before Rizzo was lowered into a steel cage in the Indian Ocean, a sixteen-foot shark ripped the cage from its cable and sent it to the ocean floor. Understandably, Rizzo announced that his shark adventures were over.

Finally, Spielberg and art director Alves agreed that some sort of mechanical shark would have to be built. Steven called a special effects wizard named Bob Mattey, who for seventeen years had been with the Disney organization, ending his career as the chief of their elaborate special effects department. At a total cost of nearly a half million dollars, Mattey built three mechanical sharks. Each was made of a polyurethane plastic. Each three-thousand-pound monster was about twenty-four-feet long and filled with air hoses and pistons to make various parts of the plastic shell move.

Each of the three mechanical sharks, quickly nicknamed Bruce by the *Jaws* crew, were used one at a time in the water. One was used for surface shots from the left, another for surface angles from the right, and the last for underwater sequences. Each Bruce was controlled by more than a dozen technicians wearing diving gear and huddled in a large cage on the ocean floor. An air hose one-hundred-feet long connected the controls on the ocean bottom with Bruce.

By the beginning of May 1974, Spielberg had moved into his temporary headquarters in a house on Martha's Vineyard. The three principal actors in the film also had arrived on the island.

Part of the reason *Jaws* is so much better than the average horror film is the trio of wonderful male actors who played the films most important roles. Chief of police Brody, who is extremely uncomfortable on the water despite the fact that he lives in a seaside resort, was played by actor Roy Scheider. Richard Dreyfuss played Hooper, an independently wealthy marine scientist who is an expert on sharks. Robert Shaw played the salty Captain Quint, who hunts, and is eventually devoured by, the killer shark in an attempt to collect a reward offered by the town.

While the director and his three main actors worked polishing and repolishing the script, preparations were made to begin filming. But from the very beginning of actual work, *Jaws* was plagued by problems. When Bruce was put in the choppy waters of the Atlantic Ocean, he promptly sank. When he was repaired and put in the water again, he exploded. The weather, like the mechanical shark, also failed to cooperate numerous times.

In addition to the three Bruces, real sharks were needed for filming also. In one case, a dead shark was needed. It would appear in shots showing local fishermen who mistakenly thought they had killed the killer shark. A number of Martha's Vineyard anglers assured Steven they could catch a large shark. But despite a salary of $100 a day, none were able to do so. Desperate for a shark and already behind schedule, Steven bought a tiger shark recently caught near Florida and had it shipped on ice to Martha's Vineyard.

During the early stages of filming, the shark hung from a hook at a dock for several days, making such a stench that townspeople in Edgartown complained bitterly. Some were so angered that they left the rotting carcasses of sharks caught near the island at the front door of producers Zanuck and Brown.

Other events on land caused problems. Much of the filming would be done in the little resort village of Chilmark on Martha's Vineyard. A tall house to be constructed for one of the movie's characters was too high for the Chilmark building codes. Finally, a $150,000 bond had to be posted by the film company guaranteeing that the house would be torn down immediately after filming was complete.

Although Martha's Vineyard is filled during the summer months with wealthy families on vacation, the film company was plagued by thefts and vandalism throughout the project. Crowds of curious islanders, fascinated by the process of filming a major motion picture and worried about its impact on the relatively small island, caused continuous problems. Spielberg was constantly asked why he was so young.

But by far the greatest problems the film crew faced were the elements themselves—especially the unpredictable Atlantic Ocean—and the mechanical Bruces. The first scene shot with Bruce was a disaster. Director Brian De Palma, a friend of Steven's, visited the island to give moral support. When he arrived, he found Steven just leaving a screening room after watching rushes of the scene with Bruce.

"It was like a wake," De Palma remembered. "Bruce's eyes crossed, and his jaws wouldn't close right."[3]

The actors, after seeing the same rushes, sat in embarrassed silence. Richard Dreyfuss finally spoke up and said, "If any of us had any sense, we'd all bail out now."[4]

Fortunately, everyone stayed through the ordeal. But many more problems arose. As the months passed, spring became summer, and the tourist season on Martha's Vineyard came into full swing. The waters of the Atlantic Ocean, virtually deserted when art director Joe Alves scouted the location in winter, were now awash with boats of every description.

Executives at Universal were becoming alarmed about the many delays in filming. Some of them suggested that the many boats be included in the shots. "We couldn't do it," Steven insisted. "You have three guys out in a rickety boat, hunting a killer shark. What kind of menace is there going to be if there is a family of four only fifty feet away, having a picnic on their sailboat?"[5]

Even when it was possible to keep pleasure boats away from the ocean set, problems with the mechanical sharks developed almost continuously. Once, Walter Cronkite was visiting Spielberg and the *Jaws* crew. For many years, Cronkite was the anchorman of the CBS television network evening news. Steven remembered how embarrassed he was to see Bruce fail, yet again, in front of one of the most highly respected people in the United States.

Walter Cronkite owned a house on Martha's Vineyard and

took a month off from his television news duties to vacation on the island. He was fascinated by the movie being filmed there and often visited the set, even when it was out on the Atlantic Ocean. Cronkite and Spielberg became friends.

One day when Cronkite was visiting, director Spielberg and his crew were testing Bruce for one of the climactic scenes in *Jaws*. The shark was supposed to jump out of the ocean and crash onto the deck of Captain Quint's boat. Instead, Bruce got tangled in its cable and floated, tail first, to the surface. Steven felt humiliated in front of the famous newscaster. Trying to ease the tension, Cronkite asked if Steven had ever considered a career in broadcasting.

Not until October, when he had already spent twice as much money as he had budgeted and was already months behind schedule, did Steven finish filming on Martha's Vineyard. During that period of nearly half a year, Steven was the only member of the company who did not leave the island even a single time. He was afraid that, had he left, he might never come back. When he did leave at last, he reportedly yelled, "I shall not return!"[6]

Spielberg did not return to Martha's Vineyard. But he was soon back on the ocean, this time in the Pacific to shoot some more final scenes. When that was finally done, there still was much more work to do.

Steven worked closely with composer John Williams to fit the musical score to the action on the screen. Films of live sharks, shot by Ron and Valerie Taylor, had to be spliced carefully into existing scenes. Film editor Verna Fields, working with Steven and mile after mile of film, carefully edited all the scenes together to give the picture a polished, final look. Particularly difficult were the many scenes shot on the ocean, which tended to reflect the many different colors of the sky.

"It's a horror film that's going to tear your guts out,"[7] Steven had boasted during the first month of filming *Jaws*. He didn't know at the time what horrors awaited the director as well. But when *Jaws* was released in the summer of 1975, the difficulties of the past year were easy to forget.

The show was a smashing success. In its initial release to theaters, *Jaws* earned more than $100 million, the first movie in history to do so. In fact, *Jaws* was the most successful movie in the history of filmmaking until George Lucas's *Star Wars* was released two years later. *Jaws* was not only tremendously successful at the box office, but most people agreed that it was a very good movie, which is not always the same as an economically successful one. It earned four Academy Award nominations, including one for best picture. Spielberg was not nominated for best director, a fact that made him feel sad.

But he did not worry about the fact for long. Well before *Jaws* was released, he was already hard at work on a new motion picture.

61

While filming *Close Encounters of the Third Kind,* Steven Spielberg (above) instructs two thousand Hindu movie extras how to raise their hands for a scene. On the first take (below), it was obvious many of the extras did not understand Steven's directions.

Left: Steven as director on an NBC-TV series entitled *Amazing Stories*

A scene from the movie *1941*

The great white shark in a scene from *Jaws* (right) and the bathers frantically leaving the water (below)

Above: Steven with two of the actors from *Jaws,* Roy Scheider and Richard Dreyfuss
Below: On the set of *I Wanna Hold Your Hand,* Steven talks with associate producer/writer Bob Gale.

Left: In 1983, the Hasty Pudding Club of Harvard University named Steven Spielberg as Man of the Year, the first nonactor to receive the honor.

Below: Steven, Harrison Ford, and Kate Capshaw at London's Heathrow Airport in 1983

Above: In London for the 1984 royal premiere of *Indiana Jones and the Temple of Doom* are, left to right: George Lucas, executive producer; Kate Capshaw and Ke Huy Quan, two of the film's stars; and director Steven Spielberg.

Below: In a crowd watching the lift-off of the space shuttle *Columbia* at Kennedy Space Center in 1983 are Steven Spielberg (center) and George Lucas (pointing).

Two scenes from *Indiana Jones and the Temple of Doom* show Indiana Jones (Harrison Ford), Short Round (Ke Huy Quan), and Willie Scott (Kate Capshaw) arriving in the village of Mayapore, India (above) and Jones and Short Round searching for an escape from the spike chamber.

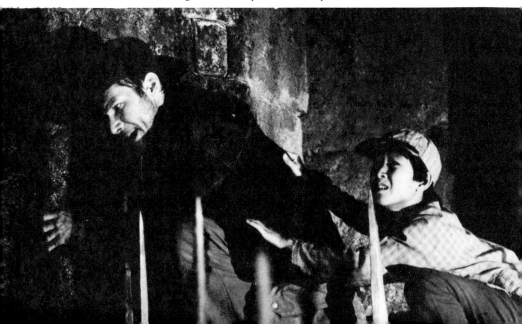

Above: A scene from *The Color Purple* with Mister (Danny Glover) and Celie (Desreta Jackson) as a young girl

Below: Steven and George Lucas place their hands and feet in cement in the forecourt of Mann's Chinese Theater in 1984.

Steven Spielberg directing *Close Encounters of the Third Kind*

Chapter 6

# ALIENS AND LOST ARKS

By the fall of 1977, *Jaws* had accumulated a worldwide income of around $400 million. Even though he had gone way over budget, Steven had spent about $8 million to film it. *Jaws*, therefore, had been enormously profitable. The success of the movie made its director, now twenty-nine years old, a celebrity and a wealthy young man.

Before *Jaws* became a national phenomenon, Steven had lived in a comfortable but relatively modest house that he shared with his dog. Soon, he moved to an area near Beverly Hills called Coldwater Canyon where he lived in a mansion with glamorous actress Amy Irving, his close friend of several years. The large home reflected Steven's youth and his fondness for toys and gadgets. It was filled with computerized games, pinball machines, and pool tables.

Even at twenty-nine, he was certainly beginning to enjoy some of the benefits of years of hard work. But the success of *Jaws*, if anything, just made him anxious to work even harder.

In the late fall of 1977, Steven's third theatrical film, *Close Encounters of the Third Kind*, was about to open in theaters across the United States. In a sneak preview given in a theater in Texas, two professional movie reviewers had managed to see the film, and had given generally bad reviews.

For the first time, Steven had directed a theatrical film for a movie studio other than Universal. *Close Encounters of the Third Kind* was made for the large but financially troubled Columbia Pictures motion picture studio. Steven's friend and fellow director John Milius accurately described what the movie meant to the studio. "It will either be the best Columbia film or it will be the last Columbia film,"[1] he noted.

It might seem surprising that a studio that recently had barely escaped financial collapse would back an expensive motion picture that eventually cost $18 million. But there were reasons. George Lucas, the man Steven had met while a college student and who soon became his partner in several films, had recently released his phenomenally successful *Star Wars*. Executives at Columbia must have hoped they could share some of *Star Wars'* success with a movie about UFOs.

Back in 1973, while still completing *The Sugarland Express*, Spielberg had made a handshake agreement with producers Michael and Julia Phillips to make a movie about unidentified flying objects. As a starting point for a script, the three people agreed to use a story idea called "Watch the Skies" that Steven had developed for a Columbia Pictures executive. In "Watch the Skies," an officer from the United

States Air Force is required to make an official cover-up of UFO sightings for the government.

Screenwriter Paul Schrader developed a script for the planned movie. Although Steven was disappointed by it, he apparently liked the title, *Close Encounters of the Third Kind*. The name refers to three levels of evidence that might be used to prove the existence of UFOs and, perhaps, extraterrestrial life-forms. Evidence of the first kind is a sighting. The second kind of evidence involves physical artifacts, such as parts of machinery from a spacecraft. The third kind, the most dramatic, is direct contact with alien beings.

The final script for *Close Encounters* was developed by Hal Barwood and Matt Robbins, who had worked on *The Sugarland Express*, and by Steven himself. Apparently, Spielberg took the lead in writing the final script.

To fill the principal roles in the film, Steven selected actor Richard Dreyfuss, with whom he had worked so successfully in *Jaws*, actress Melinda Dillon, and, playing her son, child actor Cary Guffey. In a surprising move, Spielberg also asked the famous French film director Francois Truffaut to play the role of a scientist named Lacombe. To his great surprise, Truffaut accepted, noting that he was familiar with Spielberg's work because of *Duel*. Throughout the production of *Close Encounters*, Steven had hoped that the French director of such movies as *Jules and Jim*, *Shoot the Piano Player*, and *The Wild Child* would make his own suggestions for improvements in the movie. Instead the French-man told the American, "This actor will not have ideas. I will perform your ideas."[2]

From the very beginning of actual filming in early 1976, the studio went to extraordinary lengths to keep the movie's suspenseful story line from becoming public. Although the movie was shot in locations as widely scattered as southern California, India, and Mobile, Alabama, security guards watched over most of the sets night and day to keep out anyone not directly connected with the project. Steven himself was once thrown off his own set when he forgot to bring his identification badge to work. Even Richard Dreyfuss, the star of the movie, was refused entrance to the largest set—a huge abandonded Air Force hangar in Mobile, Alabama—several times. All members of the cast and the production company were forbidden to talk about the movie in interviews.

Briefly, the story of *Close Encounters* follows a number of people who are drawn to the well-known remains of an ancient volcano in Wyoming called Devil's Tower. After seeing a number of beautifully colored UFOs, through some form of mental telepathy they begin to see the strange shape of Devil's Tower in their minds' eyes. As the various people travel to Wyoming, the U.S. government goes to elaborate efforts to keep them away from Devil's Tower. A few, including the film's stars, manage to get through the blockades, where they eventually witness the landing of a huge alien spacecraft. Some of the humans board the craft, prepared to travel far into space with alien beings who are seen for a few moments in front of the dazzling light of the spaceship.

It must have been a strange experience to act in *Close Encounters*. During much of the time, actors had to react with surprise and wonder at seeing UFOs that were not added to the film until as much as a year later. The special effects wizard hired to create the UFOs was Douglas Trumbull. About a decade earlier, Trumbull had created many of the special effects used in *2001: A Space Odyssey*, the grandfather of all the modern movies about outer space.

Working closely with director Spielberg, Trumbull used all kinds of optical machinery and techniques to make his film images of, for example, small UFOs streaking above a roadway or the huge mother ship of the final scene landing at Devil's Tower. As he himself noted, he used electronic and optical tricks to control "light on film to create the appearance of a shape when in fact no shape existed."[3]

Trumbull did build a number of objects to serve as UFOs in the film, most of them simply frames containing remote-controlled lights. The primary function of the objects he built was to hold lights. Some of these "UFOs" were photographed moving on tracks in a completely dark room. Often, the lights inside the objects were aimed directly at the camera, giving a brilliant and often distorted image. "We used that technique," Trumbull said, "in order to have those UFO objects pass over, through, or around whatever the human action was in the scene. You never really distinctly see anything except in a few very brief cuts."[4] During the final stages of putting together the movie, the film of the UFOs was combined with shots of live actors and backgrounds, making the UFOs appear where none actually existed.

The huge flying saucer that appears near the end of the movie was built in the giant airplane hangar in Mobile. It was the largest interior set ever made for a motion picture. Trumbull positioned about two thousand floodlights and six even stronger lights around the edges of the saucer. "We did a lot of experimentation," Trumbull recalled. "But the result is really spectacular. The ship is a city in the sky."[5]

Black velvet was used to cover the interior walls of the hangar and a huge hundred-foot-wide screen was used to project background images suitable for the area around Devil's Tower. In some of the final scenes, as many as fifty different photographs were used to make a single frame of the motion picture. The individual shots included such things as UFOs, stars in the night sky, people, alien beings, and the ground around the great saucer.

The aliens themselves, depicted as kindly and advanced beings, were designed by the Italian craftsman Carlo Rambaldi. At the time, he was best known as the designer of King Kong in the 1976 remake of the classic old movie. Most of the aliens were actually midget actors in costumes or models animated by simple machinery. One of the aliens, however, nicknamed Puck by Steven, had to be more complex. Puck was actually an elaborate machine inside a skin-like covering. Puck could move and even make facial expressions when technicians nearly fifty feet away pulled the proper controls.

Unlike any science fiction film before it, *Close Encounters of the Third Kind* developed a sense of wonder about the mysteries of visitors from outer space. However, the cost of such film magic was both time and money. While the movie's many special effects were still being perfected, Steven Spielberg was already hard at work on other projects.

One was a movie called *I Wanna Hold Your Hand*, created for fans of the 1960s and 1970s rock music group the Beatles. Steven was not the director of the movie but its producer. Although it was not financially successful, *I Wanna Hold Your Hand* was the first of a long list of movies produced but not directed by Spielberg. Some other motion pictures he produced in later years include *Used Cars* (1980), *Poltergeist* (1982), *Gremlins* (1984), *The Goonies* (1985), *Young Sherlock Holmes* (1985), *Back to the Future* (1985), *The Money Pit* (1986), *An American Tail* (1986), and *Innerspace* (1987).

On May 26, 1977, the day after his smash motion picture *Star Wars* opened in theaters in New York and Los Angeles, George Lucas and his wife Marcia began a vacation in Hawaii. Steven soon joined them in Honolulu. Steven and George Lucas had first met while both were students in southern California nearly a decade earlier. Now they were becoming close friends. The two built an elaborate sand castle on a Hawaiian beach to act as a good luck charm for *Star Wars*. More important, they began to discuss a joint project.

Spielberg told Lucas that he wanted someday to direct an adventure movie along the lines of the James Bond films, but Lucas claimed that he had a better idea. He told Steven a brief story about an archaeologist and playboy named Indiana Smith, later renamed Indiana Jones, who traveled all over the world looking for ancient treasures. Cliff-hanging adventure and slam-bam action would be encountered throughout the film that Lucas was planning. The story eventually became *Raiders of the Lost Ark*. It was an idea that George Lucas had been considering since 1973.

For both young filmmakers, the Hawaiian vacation was soon over. Each went on to other projects. Meanwhile, occasional discussions about the movie that eventually became *Raiders of the Lost Ark* continued.

*Close Encounters of the Third Kind* was released in the late fall of 1977. To the great relief of Steven and everyone at Columbia Pictures, the movie was a terrific success. As opposed to the two critics who panned it in the sneak pre-view in Texas, most other critics applauded the film's sense of childlike wonder in the face of unknown visitors from outer space. Many also were appreciative of the oddly happy, almost mystical acting performance of French director François Truffaut. Everyone was impressed by the film's gorgeous special effects, even those who had already seen the special effects bonanza in *Star Wars*.

The next year, 1978, Steven worked on two major projects. One was a special edition of *Close Encounters*, in which he added new scenes of the interior of the great spaceship and made other changes he hoped would improve the movie. The other was a big, expensive motion picture called *1941*.

The movie *1941* may be one of the most unhappy episodes in Spielberg's adult career. He became interested in the project when his friend and fellow director John Milius showed him the script, written by Robert Zemeckis and Bob Gale. "I gagged on it," Steven recalled about reading the original screenplay, "but I was leery. When a script is so funny that you gag, that's really the kiss of death because it usually doesn't film that way."[6] John Milius may have had similar worries. He soon gave the project to Steven to direct, although Milius kept a hand in the project as executive producer.

The movie had a $20 million budget and bankable comedic

stars including Dan Aykroyd, John Belushi, and Robert Stack. Set in Los Angeles in December of 1941, the film focuses on a much exaggerated panic that supposedly overtook the West Coast two weeks after the Japanese attack on Pearl Harbor.

As filming progressed, Steven's sense of perfection soon created difficulties. Before he was finished with the filming, he took more time than was scheduled and went millions of dollars over the already hefty budget. But there was an even greater problem.

As a movie director, Steven's experience was with highly dramatic films such as *Jaws* and *Close Encounters of the Third Kind*, in which humor was secondary to drama. In every one of his major films, he managed to create a number of very funny scenes, even at moments of high drama. But *1941* was billed as pure comedy. While directing it, he suddenly found himself unable to dream up the unending string of jokes and humorous images needed in almost every scene. Instead, he fell back on what he did best: creating drama.

Steven managed to take a funny script and make an often exciting and sometimes funny movie. But it was also very strange, without a central star or even a main locale. It did have a number of strengths. Magnificent miniature models of the Los Angeles area as it appeared in the early 1940s were skillfully worked into the live action. Although virtually all the scenes were shot in Hollywood studios, the look was stunningly realistic. And the directing was bravely experimental, especially by Hollywood standards.

By the time *1941* was set to open in the spring of 1979, Steven's two previous movies, *Jaws* and *Close Encounters*, had already grossed about $630 million. It hardly seemed possible that the stupendously successful young director was frightened of his newest creation. But he was.

"Comedy is not my forte," he confessed shortly before the debut of *1941*. "I don't know how this movie will come out. And yes, I'm scared. I'm like the Cowardly Lion, and two successes back to back have not strengthened my belief in my ability to deliver."[7] All too soon, his worst fears were realized.

The movie *1941* was as unpopular as the fateful year it made fun of. As audiences stayed away in droves during 1979, it became obvious that *1941* was the biggest bomb, at least financially, of Steven's young career. Eventually, Universal was able—barely—to get its investment money back on the project. Even that was by no means clear during *1941*'s dismal first run. But instead of sulking, Steven turned his energies to the project that he and George Lucas had been discussing for so long.

Nearly two years earlier, Steven had suggested that a young Chicago advertising copywriter named Lawrence Kasdan might be able to develop a kind of fast-paced script needed for a new movie. Kasdan had written the screenplay for a movie called *Continental Divide*, and Steven sent a copy to George Lucas. Lucas agreed with Spielberg's judgment, and Lawrence Kasdan was hired to write the new script, which he finished in August of 1978.

In January 1979, Spielberg, Lucas, and Kasdan began a series of meetings to polish the script and, in many ways, reshape it. A San Francisco filmmaker named Phil Kaufman helped by making a number of suggestions about a search for the Lost Ark of the Covenant. (According to the Bible, the stone tablets containing God's Ten Commandments were placed in the Ark of the Covenant after they were brought down from Mount Sinai.) Kaufman had a book explaining that the German Nazi dictator Adolf Hitler was intrigued by religious articles. Why not, Kaufman suggested, combine the excitement of a religious treasure hunt with the drama of World War II? In this way, the final story line for *Raiders of the Lost Ark* was gradually developed.

The hero of the movie was originally named Indiana Smith, Spielberg suggested the change to Jones because he felt Smith was too common. George Lucas had also seen Indiana Smith, now Indiana Jones, as a playboy who, during the years leading up to World War II, looted treasure and battled Nazi soldiers by day and dated beautiful women at night. But his view of Indiana Jones gradually changed. "He has to be a person we can look up to," Lucas decided at last.

"We're doing a role model for little kids, so we have to be careful. We need someone who's honest and true and trusting."[8]

Most of the final decisions about the script were made by Lucas, a few by Spielberg. By the time the script was being hammered into its final form, the two directors turned their attention to finding an actor to play the starring role of Indiana Jones. George Lucas's first choice was Tom Selleck, a handsome young actor who was just beginning a series for CBS television called *Magnum, P.I.*

There was an immediate problem. Steven Spielberg and George Lucas were the hottest young directors in Hollywood. Nearly everyone in the motion picture and television business knew that the two men, working together, would be a formidable force at the box office. CBS executives refused to give Selleck permission to make the movie, figuring that any actor Lucas and Spielberg wanted was too valuable to let go.

Next, Steven suggested Harrison Ford, the man who had played Han Solo in Lucas's two *Star Wars* movies. Ford agreed to the project, as did a young actress named Karen Allen, who played the film's adventurous leading lady.

With the script and leading players set, Spielberg and Lucas still had to finish a deal with a studio to make the picture. They negotiated with every major studio in the Los Angeles area, finally signing a contract with Paramount Pictures. The contract was an unusual one. It gave Spielberg and Lucas the chance to make an incredible amount of money. But it also included enormous penalties for going over budget.

*Raiders of the Lost Ark* would be filmed in such diverse locales as Tunisia, France, Hawaii, England, and around San Francisco. The chances of going over budget on such a globe-trotting enterprise were enormous. And Steven Spielberg had developed a reputation for spending far more than he budgeted on each of his last three movies. When filming for *Raiders of the Lost Ark* began, Lucas allowed Steven to do almost all of the directing. But he kept a careful eye on how much money was being spent.

Steven Spielberg filmed *Raiders* in seventy-three days, nearly two weeks less than the eighty-five days his friend and producer George Lucas had scheduled. It was remarkably quick for such a complex and action-packed movie. But in order to do it so quickly, Steven made a number of compromises.

One of the most famous scenes in *Raiders of the Lost Ark* takes place in Tunisia. It shows Indiana Jones being confronted by a man holding a scimitar—a large, curved sword. To audiences looking at it for the first time, it seems as though Indy and the swordsman are about to begin a lengthy battle. Indy always carried a long whip, and the stage was clearly set for a battle between a man with a whip and a man with a sword.

Working with his actors and crew, Steven developed a complicated plan for the battle. He worked out a believable way that a man with a whip could overcome a much larger man with a sword. Every part of the fight was carefully worked out, including a sequence in which Harrison Ford was backed into a wall, trying to break free by snapping his whip. Steven was excited about the elaborate battle and was anxious to begin filming it.

By the time the fight was ready to be filmed, Spielberg and the rest of the movie company were anxious to leave Tunisia. The heat was unbearable, and so were the politics. The area was filled with agents of the Palestine Liberation Organization, a sometimes violent political group determined to regain its homeland that is now a part of Israel. PLO leaders probably knew that the American motion picture crew was led by a Jewish director.

The two-man battle was scheduled to be filmed over a period of two long days. But when Harrison Ford arrived on the set for the first day of shooting, he had eaten food that did not agree with him and was painfully sick. The oppresive heat and worries of a terrorist attack made matters even worse. Steven made a snap decision.

Rather than spending two days filming the fight, Spielberg told Harrison Ford to simply draw his gun and shoot the swordsman. The result is one of the funniest scenes in *Raiders of the Lost Ark*. Instead of a long episode such as is featured in dozens of martial arts movies, the battle is over in an instant. Indiana Jones's expression shows how silly and unrealistic such long battles with exotic weapons really are. Just as important, Steven's decision allowed his crew to leave Tunisia earlier than expected.

*Raiders of the Lost Ark* set amazing new standards for nonstop action movies. Harrison Ford and Karen Allen faced such dangers as an underground room filled with more than seven thousand poisonous snakes, cruel Nazis, a treacherous monkey, poisoned food, a cave filled with deadly tarantulas, and one of the most spectacular car chases ever filmed. Although the entire movie was photographed in seventy-three days, the cost was a hefty $22 million. But it was certainly worth it.

As *Raiders of the Lost Ark* was being released in 1981, George Lucas and Steven Spielberg traveled to Hawaii to build a sand castle for good luck. It must have been a great sand castle. Within less than two years, *Raiders* had sold about $335 million worth of tickets worldwide. In that amount of time, Steven's share of the profits amounted to about $22 million, about the same amount of money spent to make the movie. He was now fabulously rich—and already hard at work on other projects.

## Chapter 7

## SPIELBERG SUMMER

In the spring of 1982, thirty-four-year-old Steven Spielberg was arguably the most successful director in Hollywood. By summer's end, there was no doubt. In between those times, the summer was his. During that season, he released two megahits, *Poltergeist* and the phenomenally successful and critically acclaimed *E.T.: The Extra-Terrestrial.*

Just two of his motion pictures, *Jaws* and *E.T.*, were destined to gross about a billion dollars. And that was before *E.T.* was released on videocassettes or presented on cable and network television. Before long, Paramount Pictures president Michael Eisner would say, "Steven Spielberg is the highest-paid human being for performing a service in the history of the world."[1] Steven Spielberg had come a long way from the youngster who was afraid of almost everything and filmed model trains crashing into each other with an 8-mm camera, or had he?

In the late spring of 1982, just as his summer blockbusters were being released, *Time* magazine reported these facts about the famous director: "He will not go into an elevator alone because he knows the thing will get stuck between floors and his whitened bones will be found two weeks later. He is a hypochondriac. He owns twelve video games and plays with them for an hour a day. He is convinced that his Malibu beach house will be undermined by waves, although it does not seem to be in danger, and when asleep there he spends arduous eight-hour nights dreaming of piling sandbags around the foundation. He will not set foot in the ocean because there are sharks out there."[2]

Just a few years later, *Rolling Stone* magazine reported a similar catalog of fears. "He's scared of elevators, dislikes roller coasters ('I prefer to see where I'm going') and hates furniture with feet ('I wait for them to walk out of the room')."[3] The article also pointed out that he was once afraid of exercise and remained frightened by bugs and the thought of having to speak in public.

One of the few things that he faced fearlessly was the task of directing a multimillion dollar motion picture, a task the rest of us might find terrifying. In fact, by the summer of 1982, he had arranged his professional life very efficiently for just that purpose. He had a suite of offices at California's MGM studios decorated with artwork from some of his movies and stocked with a number of different video games. Also, he had a growing staff of assistants he felt comfortable working with. Most were young women, perhaps not so surprising since he grew up with three younger sisters.

One of Steven's closest professional associates is Kathleen

Kennedy. The two met in 1979, when both were working on Steven's *1941*. Kathy recalled how uneasy she was the first time she met the famous director. "I was supposed to go up to his house to help him organize some special-effects shots on *1941*. I got there, and he had written stuff on napkins, on the backs of envelopes, on any piece of scrap paper he could find in the house. I spent day and night sorting the stuff out."[4]

Although she started out as an assistant to Steven, before long she was acting as a producer for some of his films. So was Frank Marshall, who produced *Raiders of the Lost Ark* and was one of the few males who worked in the Spielberg organization. "Spielberg's operation was, like, twelve women, Frank Marshall, and Steven," remembered a coworker.[5]

One woman who spent less time with Steven during the summer of 1982 was the actress Amy Irving. The pair had been engaged to marry in 1979, but the engagement was broken off, although both remained friends. But another woman who was critical to Steven's success during that summer was Melissa Mathison. She was the girlfriend, and later the wife, of actor Harrison Ford, with whom Steven had worked closely during the filming of *Raiders of the Lost Ark*. During that period, Steven struck up a friendship with Melissa, a skilled writer who had scripted the screenplay for the motion picture *The Black Stallion*.

"Melissa was one of the few people on the *Raiders* location I could talk to," Steven reminisced. "I was pouring my heart out to Melissa all the time."[6] At one point during their long talks, Steven may have recalled what the French director François Truffaut had told him during the filming of *Close Encounters of the Third Kind*.

"I like you with *keeds*," Truffaut had said in his thick French accent, "you are wonderful with *keeds*, you must do a movie just with *keeds*."[7] Steven always regarded that remark as the beginning of *E.T.: The Extra-Terrestrial*, an enchanting movie about a group of suburban kids who find a being from outer space. During the filming of *Raiders*, he asked Melissa Mathison to write a screenplay about the subject.

By the time *Raiders of the Lost Ark* was released in 1981, Steven was already hard at work on *E.T.* Once again, his work was shrouded in secrecy. So that no one would realize the story line and try to make a cheap imitation, the movie was called *A Boy's Life* during most of the time it was in production. During the earliest stages of development, Steven assembled the crew who would actually put the movie together.

For the first time, Steven acted as both producer and director for a movie. As his coproducer, he chose Kathleen Kennedy, who had helped him so much since the movie *1941*. Director of photography was Allen Daviau, the man who had operated the camera during the brief production of *Amblin'* back in Steven's student days. Melissa Mathison must have written an excellent, polished screenplay. She received sole writing credit for the movie, although Steven undoubtedly played a major role in shaping the finished story.

The human stars of the film are mostly children. Finding the young actors and actresses to fill the roles was a major task. Steven looked at about five hundred children, many of whom lived in California and were trying to become child stars, carrying professional publicity photographs with them to interviews. Steven eventually concentrated on unknown kids, although for the starring roles he ended up selecting youngsters with at least some connections to the film industry.

To play the all-important role of Elliott, the young boy who finds E.T. and protects him from the prying eyes of adults, Steven selected Henry Thomas. The child actor from Texas had appeared in one other feature film, 1982's *Raggedy Man*. His younger sister Gertie was played by Drew Barrymore, granddaughter of the famous silent movie star John Barrymore. Robert MacNaughton, the most experienced actor of the group, played Elliott's older brother Michael. The only major role for an adult was that of the children's mother, played by actress Dee Wallace.

One star of the movie, of course, has yet to be mentioned: E.T. himself. "I wanted a creature that only a mother could love," Spielberg said about his plans for E.T. "I didn't want him to be sublime or beatific, or there would be no place to go in the relationship."[8] When finally completed, E.T. was, at first glance, very ugly and even somewhat frightening. One of the almost miraculous aspects of the movie is E.T.'s ability to look strangely beautiful after audiences have become accustomed to seeing him.

Reportedly, Steven wasted about $700,000 on a crew that tried to build a mechanical E.T. and failed. In desperation, he turned to the Italian designer Carlo Rambaldi, who had created the alien nicknamed Puck in *Close Encounters of the Third Kind*. It was a logical choice, because if E.T. should resemble anyone at all, it would certainly be Puck.

Rambaldi began by building a series of clay models that Steven could film and study. When a clay model was finally approved, Rambaldi began work on a full-size mechanical E.T., about the height of a four-year-old child. First he built a skeleton of aluminum and steel. Then, using fiberglass, polyurethane, and foam rubber, he added layer after layer of muscles and skin. Each layer was attached to a mechanical control that could cause the layer to move, much like actual muscles. The controls, operated by as many as eleven technicians at one time, allowed E.T. to curve his slender finger, wrinkle his nose, move his brow, and so on.

In the movie, E.T. had to appear absolutely lifelike. A tremendous number of movements were required. Because of this, it was necessary to build several different mechanical models, each one appearing virtually identical to the others but capable of thirty different kinds of motion. One lightweight model, including mechanical and electrical controls, was bolted to the floor. It was capable of different points of movement in the face, and thirty more in the body. Another more sophisticated model had electronic controls that could operate eighty-six different points of movement. Yet another E.T., used in brief shots where walking was required, was actually a midget actor inside a costume. But the artificial E.T.s, with long extendable necks too narrow for any living actor, were used most often, to the enchantment of all concerned.

Steven had an early hint about just how successful the mechanical E.T.s would be when Henry Thomas took his first screen test with the otherworldly creation. Although the director was convinced that the young actor was nearly ideal for the part of Elliott, Steven was concerned that Henry never seemed to smile. But as soon as he saw E.T. for the first time, the young actor's eyes brightened and he began to smile. Before long, the entire cast and crew were acting just as if E.T. were a living, breathing creature from another world.

Although the movie *E.T.* relied heavily on the masterful creations of Carlo Rambaldi, it was otherwise unusually lacking in special optical effects and trick photography. Some special effects were created by George Lucas's Industrial Light and Magic company, but they were relatively few in number.

Spielberg explained that he wanted to avoid photographic tricks as much as possible in filming E.T. He tried to develop the same spirit that young Elliott felt when, at one point in the movie, he says, "This is reality."

Working on *E.T.* in 1981 and the first half of 1982, Steven worried constantly that the alien's character was too gentle and feminine to be of much interest to males in the audience. Melissa Mathison constantly reassured him that everyone would be pleased by *E.T.* But Steven continued to worry, finally relaxing after giving up all hopes of pleasing men and boys.

For the first time since his days as a child shooting 8-mm film, he did not create storyboards for the entire picture. "I began storyboarding," he remembers, "then after about two weeks, when we had about half the film storyboarded, I sort of stopped and said, 'I really want to play this one by ear. I'd like to kind of wing this one and see what happens.'"9

Despite the worries and changes in plans of its director, *E.T.: The Extra-Terrestrial* was completed before the start of summer 1982. In the end, millions of moviegoers would have to decide for themselves about E.T.

But *E.T.* was not the only movie Steven was readying for the summer of 1982. The other, a far less gentle movie, was called *Poltergeist*. If *E.T.* was a sweet dream, then *Poltergeist* was a nightmare!

"Poltergeist" is a German word which means, literally,

"noisy ghosts." In the movie, evil spirits seem to call out to a five-year-old girl, played by Heather O'Rourke, from inside a television set. Before long, she is carried away to another world in scenes filled with terror. Her parents, played by Craig T. Nelson and JoBeth Williams, try desperately to save her. They finally succeed only with the help of a psychic lady played by Beatrice Straight.

Like hundreds of other movies designed to scare audiences right out of their shoes, *Poltergeist*, at its simplest, is just a ghost story. But it is a well-acted one filled with magnificent special effects. It also seems to have a message, both serious and comic. Ghosts who communicate through a television set threaten the life of a little girl. They seem to come alive in the wee hours of the morning, when stations have left the air and only static is shown on the television screen. The message seems to be this: if you never turn off your TV set, beware!

Steven Spielberg did not direct *Poltergeist*. Instead, he acted as producer with Frank Marshall, and as screenwriter with two others. But it is clear that Steven oversaw the project from beginning to end. He was constantly dropping in on the set, watching, and often changing scenes directed by the film's official director, Tobe Hooper. Like *E.T.*, *Poltergeist* was finished by the start of the 1982 summer season.

The release of the two blockbuster motion pictures created yet another phenomenal summer for Steven Spielberg. *Pol-*

tergeist did well enough to gladden the hearts and fatten the wallets of many people at MGM, the studio that distributed it. But *E.T.* became a national phenomenon soon after Universal released it. *E.T.* earned a cool half billion dollars or so in its first run, the richest take of any movie in history, easily surpassing Steven's own *Jaws* and even George Lucas's *Star Wars* movies.

*E.T.* and *Poltergeist* were remarkably profitable. Both were completed on time and under budget. Together, the two films cost about $20 million, less than the cost of *Close Encounters* alone. Movie fans, hardened critics, and even cost-conscious motion picture company accountants were in love with Steven Spielberg. "E.T. phone home," a line of dialog from the movie, became a catchphrase of the summer. Soon, E.T. dolls, toys, and posters were selling briskly in stores everywhere, with Steven Spielberg enjoying some of the profits from every sale. He had earned another huge fortune.

As *E.T.* fever reached its height during the summer of 1982, Spielberg was involved in a tragedy. For some time, he and John Landis (director of *The Blues Brothers* and *American Werewolf in London*) had been acting as coproducers for a motion picture called *Twilight Zone: The Movie*, based on an old television series by Rod Serling.

The *Twilight Zone* film had an unusual format. It was actually a series of four different stories directed by four different directors. Steven Spielberg and John Landis each directed one segment. The other two stories were directed by Joe Dante (who later directed two Spielberg-produced motion pictures, *Gremlins* in 1984 and *Innerspace* in 1987) and by George Miller, an Australian who became famous for his *Mad Max* films.

The *Twilight Zone* story Steven directed was called "Kick the Can," a tale of old people who are given the gift of youth. Many people do not consider "Kick the Can" one of Steven's better works, but at least the filming was relatively uneventful. The same could not be said of John Landis's segment.

John Landis wrote the screenplay for his *Twilight Zone* segment, which was about a man (played by the actor Vic Morrow) who disliked many groups of people, including Jews, blacks, and Asians. In the *Twilight Zone*, the hateful character finds himself carried into a number of situations in which members of those groups suffer from discrimination.

One of those situations was the Vietnam War. During the month of June 1982, director Landis established a set to look much like a scene from the Asian war. In one shot, Vic Morrow and two child actors were running from a helicopter, with bombs exploding all around them.

On June 23, a disaster occurred. Flying too close to an explosion, the helicopter was damaged and went out of control, landing on top of Morrow and the two children. All three actors were killed. The tragedy set off a storm of controversy. It was soon shown that the children were acting in violation of a number of California's child labor laws. John Landis and a number of Warner Bros. employees faced lengthy investigations and stiff fines.

About a year after the accident, Landis and four others were indicted. Landis was accused of involuntary manslaughter, a legal term indicating that prosecutors for the state of California felt that he should have been able to prevent the tragic accident.

For a time, even Steven Spielberg was under suspicion. Although he had not directed the segment, he, like John Landis, was serving as a producer for the movie. More important, a member of the film's crew reported that he had seen Spielberg on the set on June 23, shortly before the accident, a charge Steven vigorously denied. After a lengthy investigation, Spielberg was completely cleared of any wrongdoing. But John Landis faced a legal struggle that lasted for nearly five years. In 1987, a California jury finally decided that he was innocent of the criminal charges filed against him. But the sad story served as a reminder to everyone in Hollywood that safety was critically important in movie production, just as in every other form of work.

Steven must have felt bad for fellow-director Landis during his struggle. The two men were friends. During the making of Landis's highly successful 1980 film, *The Blues Brothers*, Steven made a rare acting appearance. Among the final, frantic scenes of the movie, he plays the Cook County clerk eating a sandwich who receives a check from the Blues Brothers. His three brief lines are: "Can I help you?" and "Right" and, finally, "And here is your receipt."

But in far less happy times, there was little Steven could do to lessen the tragedy caused by the accident on the *Twilight Zone* set. By January 1983, he was already at work with his old friend George Lucas planning a sequel to *Raiders of the Lost Ark*. Steven's movies, and his personal life as well, would soon be taking off in entirely new directions.

Steven and his wife Amy Irving arriving at the opening of *The Color Purple*

# Chapter 8

# THE COLOR OF LIFE

In 1983, Steven Spielberg's one-time fiancée Amy Irving was in India working on a movie. The actress recalled what happened when "one night, in front of three friends, I made a wish. I said, 'I wish I'd have a visitor, and I want it to be Steven.' Later that night my assistant came to me and said, 'Steven arrives in the morning.'"[1] He was flying to India to look at possible locations for a new movie. Once again, Steven Spielberg and George Lucas were teaming up to make an Indiana Jones movie, a sequel to *Raiders of the Lost Ark*. The new movie would be called *Indiana Jones and the Temple of Doom*.

Rather than hope that Steven would meet her on the set of her movie, Amy decided to surprise him at the airport. It must have been a fine meeting. "From that moment," she said, "I knew. Now we're really in love. And here I am with the Prince of Hollywood. I guess that makes me the Princess."[2] A few years later, in 1985, Steven and Amy were married. Their son, Max, was born the same year. The family lived in Steven's Coldwater Canyon mansion, which they often called "the house that Jaws built."

But while the romance was growing once again, Steven

Spielberg had a few other projects on his mind. First, of course, was the sequel to *Raiders of the Lost Ark*, which had brought him to India in the first place.

Spielberg had always been leery of making sequels. After the tremendous success of *Jaws*, he turned down the opportunity to do another shark story. He had nothing to do with *Jaws II*, or with *Jaws 3-D*, or with 1987's *Jaws: the Revenge*. But after some thought, he eventually decided to do *Indiana Jones and the Temple of Doom*. One of the principal reasons undoubtedly was his eagerness to once again work with his friend and fellow filmmaker, George Lucas.

For the most part, George Lucas developed the fairly complex plot for the movie, which was set in 1935, a year before the start of action in *Raiders of the Lost Ark*. The actual screenplay was written by Gloria Katz and Willard Huyck. In January of 1983, Steven began his planning for the work, which went into production midyear.

Starring with Harrison Ford were two actors new to the *Indiana Jones* films. Former schoolteacher Kate Capshaw played a singer named Willie Scott. Child actor Ke Huy Quan played the role of a worldly-wise kid called Short Round.

In the movie, the characters are confronted with an astounding series of dangerous encounters. In the opening scene, Indiana Jones is poisoned and must get the antidote held by dangerous hoodlums. Soon, the stars find themselves in a plane without a pilot, sliding down the side of a mountain, faced with a dinner featuring live eels and chilled monkey brains, and chased by scores of people in a violent religious sect, to name a few of their many perils.

*Indiana Jones and the Temple of Doom* was released by Paramount Pictures in May of 1984. While millions of people swarmed to movie houses throughout the U.S. and much of the world to see it, a controversy arose. More than any other Steven Spielberg film, at least since *Jaws, Temple of Doom* was surprisingly, even shockingly, violent. In one scene, a demented priest rips the heart—still beating—out of a living man and drops his body into a hole filled with bubbling lava.

For a good many critics, it was too much. Many complained about such graphic violence in a movie aimed, at least in part, at children. A number of critics suggested that the dangerous but good-humored fun of *Raiders of the Lost Ark* had somehow been twisted out of proportion in the sequel. Even Spielberg admitted that he would not allow a ten-year-old child to see the movie.

The violence of *Temple of Doom* sent shock waves through much of the Hollywood movie industry. It resulted in an entirely new classification for motion pictures.

For years, Hollywood studios had been using a rating system to help parents establish which movies would be suitable for children. G stood for general audiences, indicating that a movie was suitable for people of all ages. Movies rated

PG—which stands for parental guidance—were understood to be suitable for children if their parents approved. The classification R indicated films restricted to people over seventeen or children accompanied by a parent or guardian. Movies rated X were for adults only. Because of the violence in *Indiana Jones and the Temple of Doom*, a new classification called PG-13 was developed by people in the motion picture industry. Movies with the new rating were considered suitable only for children over the age of thirteen whose parents approved of their seeing the film.

Moviegoers hardly seemed to mind the flap over the violence in the movie. They flocked to see it in near record-breaking numbers. "*Raiders* films are pure escapism and have nothing to do with the real world," Steven said around the time of the *Temple of Doom* premiere. "They're just a lot of fun to make. If there's a third one, well, I would hate to see anyone else direct it."[3] It is hard to imagine that anyone else would dare, unless it were George Lucas. Despite the controversy over the violence, *Temple of Doom* soon became one of the top ten highest grossing movies of all time. Steven Spielberg had earned yet another multimillion dollar fortune.

A year later, in 1985, *Time* magazine reported an astounding fact. Of the top ten highest money-making films of all time, Steven Spielberg had directed four. *E.T.* was still the box office champion. *Jaws* was fifth, *Raiders of the Lost Ark* was seventh, and in eighth place was *Indiana Jones and the*

*Temple of Doom*. In 1987, records showed that of the film rentals of the six major U.S. film companies overseas, *E.T.* and *Jaws* led the list in sales.

Even at the time of the *Temple of Doom* premiere, Steven was living like the astonishingly rich man he was. He owned a mansion in Los Angeles, a magnificent beach house on the ocean in Malibu, and enjoyed exclusive use of a lavish apartment in Trump Tower, a new and exclusive building in New York City. His favorite car was a $45,000 Porsche convertible.

As if this were not enough, he was also in the process of getting a brand new office. And what an office it was!

"There are very few things Steven could ask of us that he could not get," said Steven's old friend Sidney Sheinberg, president of the company that owns Universal Pictures. "There is no one that we are more anxious to please."[4] After working in offices at Warner Bros. for some time, Steven decided that he would like to come home to the studio that produced his first motion pictures, as well as *Jaws* and *E.T.* Officials at Universal were more than happy to oblige.

Based on Spielberg's own designs, the company built a southwestern-style mansion on a distant corner of the Universal lot. The building was the new home away from home for Steven, Kathleen Kennedy, Frank Marshall, and the rest of the fifteen-member film company called Amblin' Entertainment. The unusual headquarters has, of course, an electronic game room, as well as a movie theater, two film editing rooms, a kitchen complete with a permanent chef, a gym, a steam room, and lots of different offices. The rooms are filled with Indian pottery, Tiffany lamps, and memorabilia from Spielberg's films.

Outside the stucco building is a stream fed by a rushing waterfall and stocked with exotic Japanese koi, a kind of black and silver fish. A wooden bridge crosses the stream. Near the front entrance is a wishing well where Bruce, the mechanical shark from *Jaws*, pokes his nose out of the water. "What can I say?" Steven once said about his new working home. "This is the most amazing gift I've ever received."[5]

It is also a setting, apparently, that gives filmmakers a chance to do work that is sometimes stunning. Beginning in 1984, a number of highly successful films were developed in the new headquarters, many produced by the team of Steven Spielberg, Frank Marshall, and Kathleen Kennedy.

Back in 1982, when Steven was looking for a writer to work on *Indiana Jones and the Temple of Doom*, the agent for a twenty-three-year-old writer named Chris Columbus submitted a screenplay called *Gremlins*. Steven read the script and thought it was horrible, but liked the idea about a cute little animal that turns into a monster—and all too soon many monsters—when not treated properly. After nine Columbus rewrites, the script became the basis for the first hit movie by the executive producing team of Spielberg, Marshall, and Kennedy. *Gremlins*, like *Indiana Jones and the Temple of Doom*, was released in May 1984. Although some critics also complained of the violence in it, moviegoers hardly seemed to mind, making it a major hit for Amblin' Entertainment.

Chris Columbus also wrote the screenplay for another popular film, *The Goonies*, which was released in 1985. Before long, Columbus was working as a director, although not for Amblin' Entertainment. His *Adventures in Baby Sitting* became the surprise comedy hit of the 1987 summer season, hot competition for Amblin's own summer offering, *Innerspace*.

One of the most imaginative and enjoyable of the Amblin' producers' films was 1985's *Back to the Future*, starring Michael J. Fox, Crispin Glover, Lea Thompson, and Christopher Lloyd. In the movie, a teenager played by Fox travels back in time and meets his own parents, almost destroying himself in the process. *Back to the Future* was a tremendous hit, in movie houses during its first run, and in rental stores when it was released on videocassettes.

Only a few Amblin' films have failed to bring in box office gold. *Young Sherlock Holmes* was released in 1985 to half-empty movie houses throughout the country. The people who saw it often enough believed it was a well-crafted and entertaining movie, but too few tickets were sold to make it a financial success.

After some delays *The Money Pit* was released in 1986 to mixed reviews and lackluster attendance. Starring Tom Hanks and Shelley Long, the movie portrays the unending disasters faced by a young couple who buy a big old house in poor repair.

An animated cartoon from the same year, *An American Tail*, also received mixed reviews from critics, although many youngsters adored it. The feature-length cartoon told about a family of mice who moved to the United States around the time the Statue of Liberty was being built in New York harbor. The movie was released on videocassettes in 1987. In its October 31 edition of that year, *TV Guide* reported that *An American Tail* was, at the time, the third most frequently requested tape in video rental stores.

A Spielberg production that was far less successful than anticipated was his television series called *Amazing Stories*. Presented on the NBC television network from 1985 to 1987, *Amazing Stories* was one of the most expensive continuing series ever made for television. NBC paid a record-shattering fee of nearly one million dollars to show each episode, but the series was consistently beaten out in the ratings by CBS's *Murder, She Wrote*, starring Angela Lansbury. When programmers moved *Amazing Stories* to a different day, the ratings failed to improve.

Part of the problem with the series was that it was an anthology. Steven hired dozens of different writers and directors to develop the series. Naturally, some of the shows were better than others. Although some of the productions were very good indeed, the constantly shifting themes and styles evident from episode to episode failed to attract a large television audience. Much ballyhooed as Steven Spielberg's triumphant return to television, even though he directed only a handful of episodes, the series ended in 1987.

All of these films, as well as all but a few of the *Amazing Stories* episodes, were produced, but not directed, by Steven Spielberg, usually in association with his Amblin' Entertainment crew. But in July of 1987, a film that was directed by Spielberg, *The Color Purple*, was released for the first time on videocassettes. Millions of people saw the movie when it appeared in movie theaters in 1985. In 1987, millions more saw it on television sets wired to videocassette recorders. For Steven Spielberg, the film was a radical departure from his usual stories filled with fantasy, science fiction, and high adventure.

The movie is based on the book *The Color Purple* by the novelist Alice Walker, who won the Pulitzer Prize for fiction in 1983. Walker's book is a series of fictional letters addressed to God by a young black woman named Celie who grows up in the early 1900s in the southern United States. Later in the book, other letters from Celie's sister Nettie, who went to Africa as a missionary, are presented also. Through the letters, readers learn of the hard, sad life Celie leads, first at the hands of her cruel stepfather, and later through her equally unkind husband.

Much of the lengthy and relatively complex story is almost unbearably sad. Celie's stepfather abuses her terribly in just about every way imaginable. One of the few bright spots in her young life is her happy relationship with her beloved sister Nettie. Soon, Celie's stepfather forces her to become the wife of a stiffly humorless and sometimes violent man called "Mister." As Celie settles into her miserable life with Mister, sister Nettie runs away from home to join her in Mister's house. But their joy at being reunited is short-lived. Mister soon throws Nettie out of the house. Knowing that the end is coming, Nettie manages to teach Celie how to read and write a bit before the heart-rending separation comes.

"Write," Celie calls in desperation to her sister as she runs away from a hail of rocks thrown at her by Mister. Then the years pass slowly. For decades Nettie writes long letters to her sister. But Mister will not allow Celie to read or even see the letters. Instead, he hides them in the house. Celie eventually finds some comfort with a number of different women, especially a blues singer named Shug Avery and an in-law (the wife of her husband's son through a previous marriage) named Sophia.

With the help of Shug, Celie eventually manages to grow more independent of her husband. The two women at last find the hidden letters from Celie's sister Nettie, which for twenty years Mister had hidden under a loose board in his house. With great excitement, Celie reads about her sister's eventually tragic experiences in Africa, where she traveled with missionaries. In the end, Celie is reunited with her long-lost sister and with her own two children, who had been taken away from her when she was a young girl. She finds the strength to leave her cruel husband to fend for himself, which he does with considerable difficulty.

When the novel *The Color Purple* was published, many people were moved by Celie's struggles and her hard-won independence from the men who treated her so badly. But there was also controversy. A number of people objected to the novel's depiction of black men—all the important male roles in the book—as cruel and violent. But the controversy was nothing compared to that developed by Steven Spielberg's version.

Of the many people who admired the novel *The Color Purple*, one was Steven's friend and Amblin' Entertainment coworker Kathy Kennedy. She persuaded him to read the book.

"When I read it," Steven reported, "I loved it; I cried and cried at the end. But I didn't think I would ever develop it as a project."[6] After some time, and considerable urging from Kennedy, he finally changed his mind. By the time he did, Warner Bros. was already planning a movie version of the book. Musician and composer Quincy Jones, the force behind a number of Michael Jackson's hits as well as the famous "We Are the World" charity record and video, was already serving as a producer on the project. When he expressed interest, Steven was immediately offered the chance to direct the movie. But there were a number of problems to overcome.

The novel was written as a long series of letters. That approach, as good as it was for the book, would never work in a movie. A Dutch writer named Menno Meyjes finally managed to transform the letters from the novel into a more traditional screenplay. Another problem was finding actors and actresses to fill the challenging roles in the nearly all-black cast.

At the suggestion of author Alice Walker, the starring role—Celie as an adult—was given to a comedienne and stage actress named Whoopi Goldberg who had never before appeared in a movie. The choice was all the more remarkable since Whoopi had wanted the much smaller role of Sophia, eventually won by talk-show hostess Oprah Winfrey. Amazingly, Steven had to talk Whoopi Goldberg into accepting the starring role. Still, she resisted. "Then," she said, "I realized I was saying no to Steven Spielberg, who wanted me for the lead."

Soon enough, the actress realized she would be happy for any role in the movie—even the lead. "Honey," she soon said, "in *The Color Purple*, I'd play the dirt."[7] Instead, she gave a wonderful performance as Celie, the shy, awkward woman who finally rises above the men who treat her so badly. Other starring roles in the film were filled by Danny Glover as Mister, and Margaret Avery as Shug. Desreta Jackson played Celie as a young girl.

When the movie version of *The Color Purple* was completed, the result was a beautiful, gripping, and, at least according to some critics, flawed motion picture. Steven and director of photography Allen Daviau painted stunningly beautiful portraits of the rural South as it would have appeared in the first half of the twentieth century. The performances of the film's stars, especially Whoopi Goldberg, Danny Glover, Oprah Winfrey, and a number of child actresses, were extremely memorable.

But the old controversies about the novel—and some new ones about the movie—arose almost immediately. Angered by the film's portrayal of black men, a number of different civil rights organizations established picket lines in front of motion picture houses showing it. The main objection, of course, was to the mean spirit of male characters like Celie's stepfather and her husband Mister.

But the movie brought about a new controversy as well. The homes in which Celie lived, first with her stepfather and especially later with Mister, were unusually spacious and comfortable for blacks in the early twentieth century. Then, too, scenes of meals being served showed plentiful supplies of meat, vegetables, and grain. There was hardly any indication, some critics claimed, of the grinding poverty that led so many black men to less than perfect behavior. In two scenes in the movie, one frightening, the other sad, the effects of discrimination on black people and lack of understanding by whites is clearly shown. But the brief scenes do not seem to thoroughly account for the behavior of most of the men in the movie.

Late in 1986, after much of the controversy over the movie had at last subsided, the novel's author, Alice Walker, published a fascinating article in *Ms* magazine. Written as a letter to an African-American friend named Mpinga, Walker analyzed the criticisms made about *The Color Purple*.

In her article, Walker paid particular attention to the cruel character of Celie's husband, Mister. Her analysis sheds light on a fact that must have been missed by a good many people. "I have not, by any means," she wrote, "read or even seen all the negative reviews of Mister's character and its implications for blacks in America. However, in the ones I have read, I've been struck by the absence of any analysis of who, in fact, Mister is. Nobody, no critic, that is, has asked this character, 'Boy, who your peoples?'"

"In the novel and in the movie (even more in the movie because you can *see* what color people are) it is clear that Mister's father is part white; this is how Mister comes by his rundown plantation house. It belonged to his grandfather, a white man and a slave owner. Mister learns how to treat women and children from his father, Old Mister. Who did Old Mister learn from? Well, from Old Master, his slave-owning father, who treated Old Mister's mother and Old Mister (growing up) as slaves, *which they were.*"[8]

Walker's explanation makes it easier to understand the reason that some male characters in *The Color Purple*, especially Mister, act so violently toward the women in their lives. The behavior they displayed was really the violence of the white slave owner—who treated human beings as just so many pieces of property—that was passed down through generations of victims. This explanation may not satisfy every critic of Alice Walker's book or of Steven Spielberg's film. But it is too bad that the controversy generated so much heat and so little light. Alice Walker seemed satisfied with the movie version of her book. She was paid to be a consultant for the movie throughout the project. It is exceptionally unlikely that Spielberg often ignored her advice.

The movie version of *The Color Purple* created one more strange controversy. The film was nominated for nearly a dozen different Academy Awards, and won virtually nothing. Spielberg was not even nominated for best director, although the movie was nominated for best picture.

It is one of the oddities of Steven's still relatively young career that he has never won an Oscar for directing. Steven doesn't try to hide his disappointment over his lack of awards. "I don't think the Oscars are silly at all," he has said.

"I'd like to win one for what I thought was my best work but I'd take it any time."[9]

Although he did not win an Oscar, Steven was finally honored at the Academy Award ceremonies during the spring of 1987. At the ceremony that year, he was given the Irving G. Thalberg Memorial Award for career achievements. The thirty-nine-year-old director must have been one of the youngest recipients of the prize, usually reserved for much older people. During his acceptance speech, Steven noted that movies had been the literature of his life, but called for filmmakers to give renewed respect to the importance of written words in American culture.

In December of 1987, theaters across the country began showing the first new film directed by Steven Spielberg since *The Color Purple*. While his wife Amy was on location in New York starring in another movie under production, Steven's *Empire of the Sun* was announced in a flurry of print reviews and broadcast media stories. Like *The Color Purple*, the new movie concentrated on a realistic portrayal of human beings in difficult circumstances, rather than on beings from outer space and special effects.

Based on a novel by J.G. Ballard, *Empire of the Sun* tells the story of a wealthy British schoolboy who lives in the Chinese city of Shanghai during the early years of World War II. The life of the nine-year-old boy, played by Christian

Bale, is thrown into chaos when the city is attacked and conquered by Japanese soldiers in 1941. Trying to escape with his parents through the smoky streets of Shanghai, the boy at one tragic moment reaches for a favorite toy airplane instead of his mother's hand. He is soon lost in the crowds of panicked residents and running soldiers. Unable to find his parents, he returns to his deserted home, where he rides his bicycle through empty rooms and eats canned food.

The boy soon begins wandering through the shadowy underworld of the conquered city in search of his lost family. Just as he is learning the savage skills needed to survive in his bleak new world, he is captured by the Japanese and placed in a prison camp where he spends the remainder of the war years.

Like the other prisoners, he suffers terribly. But even in the prison camp, he finds moments of happiness. He enjoys, sometimes, a friendship with an American sailor, played by the actor John Malkovich, who displays a sharp wit and sometimes questionable behavior. The boy is also mothered and befriended by a married woman who, for a time, takes the place of the family he has lost, and even the girlfriend he never had.

The boy, who is both suddenly and gradually becoming a man, finds yet another object of joy amidst his brutal circumstances. His prison is located next to an airfield. Always fascinated by airplanes, he watches the takeoffs and landings with awe, feeling respect for the Japanese pilots who soared into the sky. But it is an American airplane that ends his imprisonment. Near the conclusion of the two-hour-and-twenty-five-minute film, the young man, now about thirteen years old, sees the brilliant flash of the atomic bomb over the Japanese city of Hiroshima. Soon, airplanes are dropping cans of food and packages of cigarettes to the starving prisoners in the camp. World War II was over.

In *Empire of the Sun*, Spielberg worked with many of the same people he had worked with in earlier motion pictures. Allen Daviau, the same man who had helped him film *Amblin'* and *E.T.*, was the director of photography. John Williams once again wrote the musical score. And helping Steven produce the movie were his old friends and coworkers, Kathleen Kennedy and Frank Marshall. Writer Tom Stoppard, a noted playwright, adapted J.G. Ballard's novel for the screen.

If *The Color Purple* and *Empire of the Sun* are any indications, Steven Spielberg's interests in filmmaking seem to be changing. Imaginary monsters and UFOs created by special effects wizards are becoming more scarce in his movies. But they are making room for something perhaps even more exciting: the realistic adventures, both grand and tragic, of ordinary human beings. There is magic in those stories as well.

Of course, as the head of his own movie company, Spielberg had not forgotten his roots. At about the same time *Empire of the Sun* was released, Amblin' Entertainment's *batteries not included* premiered in movie houses around the nation. Directed by Mathew Robbins, the film has an unusual name, without the capital letters found in most titles. In the movie, the operators of a small cafe, played by Hume Cronyn and Jessica Tandy, help some people who live in a run-down apartment house battle real estate developers. But the plot takes a classic Spielberg twist when tiny aliens from outer space become involved in the struggle. George Lucas's Industrial Light and Magic company produced many of the movie's lively special effects.

"I'm intolerably happy,"[10] Steven said back in 1984. Three years later, in December 1987, the veteran director celebrated his fortieth birthday. With a loving family and a string of hit movies—his lifelong dream—already to his credit, it is hard to imagine that he is anything but happy still.

# ACKNOWLEDGMENTS

**The editors would like to acknowledge use of excerpted material from the following works:**

Excerpts from THE JEWISH MOTHERS' HALL OF FAME by Fred Bernstein. Copyright © 1986 by Fred Bernstein. Reprinted by permission of DOUBLEDAY a division of Bantam, Doubleday, Dell Publishing Group, Inc.

"Sand Castles" by Todd McCarthy, © 1985, *Film Comment* (May/June 1982): 59.

Reprinted from SKYWALKING: THE LIFE AND FILMS OF GEORGE LUCAS by Dale Pollack. Copyright © 1983 by Dale Pollack. Used by permission of Harmony Books, a division of Crown Publishers, Inc.

"Spielberg tells why he's films' most successful director," by Gene Siskel. Reprinted by permission: Tribune Media Services.

From THE MOVIE BRATS: HOW THE FILM GENERATION TOOK OVER HOLLYWOOD by Michael Pye and Lynda Myles. Copyright © 1979 by Michael Pye and Lynda Myles. Reprinted by permission of Henry Holt and Company, Inc.

By Michael Sragow from *Rolling Stone Magazine*. By Straight Arrow Publishers, Inc. © 1982. All Rights Reserved. Reprinted by permission.

Excerpt from "In the Closet of the Soul" by Alice Walker. Published in *Ms*, November 1986. Reprinted by permission of The Wendy Weil Agency, Inc. Copyright © 1986 by Alice Walker.

Copyright 1975, 1977, 1979, 1981, 1982, 1985 Time Inc. All rights reserved. Reprinted by permission from TIME.

Copyright 1974, 1977, 1984, 1985 by Newsweek, Inc. All rights reserved. Reprinted by permission.

# FOOTNOTES

Chapter 1. THE LITTLEST DIRECTOR
1. "The Autobiography of Peter Pan," *Time* (July 15, 1985): 63
2. Ibid.
3. Michael Sragow, "Will Hollywood's Mr. Perfect Ever Grow Up?" *Rolling Stone* (July 19/August 2, 1984): 35
4. From the book, *The Jewish Mothers' Hall of Fame* by Fred Bernstein. Doubleday & Company, Inc. Reprinted in "Present at the Creation," *People Weekly* (May 5, 1986): 100
5. Ibid.
6. "I Dream for a Living," *Time* (July 15, 1985): 55
7. "The Autobiography of Peter Pan," *Time* (July 15, 1985): 62
8. *The Jewish Mothers' Hall of Fame* by Fred Bernstein. Reprinted in "Present at the Creation," *People Weekly*: 98
9. "The Autobiography of Peter Pan," *Time* (July 15, 1985): 62
10. Ibid.
11. "I Dream for a Living," *Time* (July 15, 1985): 56
12. Ibid.
13. "Close Encounter with Spielberg," *Newsweek* (November 21, 1977): 98
14. *The Jewish Mothers' Hall of Fame* by Fred Bernstein. Reprinted in "Present at the Creation," *People Weekly*: 98
15. Ibid.
16. "The Autobiography of Peter Pan," *Time* (July 15, 1985): 62
17. "The Autobiography of Peter Pan," *Time* (July 15, 1985): 63

Chapter 2. ON TO CALIFORNIA
1. "Steve's Summer Magic," *Time* (May 31, 1982): 57
2. Todd McCarthy, "Sand Castles," *Film Comment* (May/June 1982): 59
3. "The Autobiography of Peter Pan," *Time* (July 15, 1985): 61

4. "Hard Riders," *Newsweek* (April 8, 1974): 87
5. "I Dream for a Living," *Time* (July 15, 1985): 57
6. *The Jewish Mothers' Hall of Fame* by Fred Bernstein. Reprinted in "Present at the Creation," *People Weekly*: 100
7. Todd McCarthy, "Sand Castles," *Film Comment* (May/June 1982): 54
8. "The Autobiography of Peter Pan," *Time* (July 15, 1985): 63
9. "I Dream for a Living," *Time* (July 15, 1985): 57
10. Ibid.
11. Gene Siskel, "Spielberg tells why he's films' most successful director," *Chicago Tribune* (June 6, 1982): Arts & Entertainment section
12. "I Dream for a Living," *Time* (July 15, 1985): 57

Chapter 3. AMBLIN' INTO HOLLYWOOD
1. Dale Pollack, *SKYWALKING: The Life and Films of George Lucas* (New York: Harmony Books, 1983): 68-69
2. "Close Encounter with Spielberg," *Newsweek* (November 21, 1977): 98
3. Michael Sragow, "Will Hollywood's Mr. Perfect Ever Grow Up?" *Rolling Stone* (July 19/August 2, 1984): 35
4. Ibid.
5. "I Dream for a Living," *Time* (July 15, 1985): 56
6. Michael Sragow, "Will Hollywood's Mr. Perfect Ever Grow Up?" *Rolling Stone* (July 19/August 2, 1984): 35
7. Ibid.
8. Ibid.
9. Ibid.

Chapter 4. THE SPIELBERG EXPRESS
1. Michael Pye and Lynda Myles, *The Movie Brats* (New York: Holt, Rinehart and Winston, 1979): 227

2. Donald Mott and Cheryl Saunders, *Steven Spielberg* (Boston: G.K. Hall & Co., 1986): 25 (The authors in a footnote attribute the quote to Mitch Tuchman in his article "Close Encounters with Steven Spielberg," *Film Comment*, January-February 1978, p. 53.)
3. Michael Pye and Lynda Myles, *The Movie Brats* (New York: Holt, Rinehart and Winston, 1979): 227-228
4. Ibid., 228
5. Ibid., 231

Chapter 5. SHARK SUMMER
1. Michael Pye and Lynda Myles, *The Movie Brats* (New York: Holt, Rinehart and Winston, 1979): 235
2. Ibid., 235-236
3. "Summer of the Shark," *Time* (June 23, 1975): 49
4. Ibid.
5. Ibid., 50
6. Donald Mott and Cheryl Saunders, *Steven Spielberg* (Boston: G.K. Hall & Co., 1986): 52
7. "Hunting the Shark," *Newsweek* (June 24, 1974): 80

Chapter 6. ALIENS AND LOST ARKS
1. Michael Pye and Lynda Myles, *The Movie Brats* (New York: Holt, Rinehart and Winston, 1979): 241
2. "He Was the Movies," *Film Comment* (February 1985): 41
3. "Wizard of Special Effects," *Newsweek* (November 21, 1977): 99
4. "A City in the Sky," *Time* (November 7, 1977): 105
5. Ibid.
6. "Animal House Goes to War," *Time* (April 16, 1979): 97
7. Ibid.

8. Dale Pollack, *SKYWALKING: The Life and Films of George Lucas* (New York: Harmony Books, 1983): 224

Chapter 7. SPIELBERG SUMMER
1. "The Wizard of Wonderland," *Newsweek* (June 4, 1984): 79
2. "Staying Five Moves Ahead," *Time* (May 31, 1982): 58
3. Michael Sragow, "Will Hollywood's Mr. Perfect Ever Grow Up?" *Rolling Stone* (July 19/August 2, 1984): 38
4. Ibid.
5. Ibid.
6. Michael Sragow, "A Conversation with Spielberg," *Rolling Stone* (July 22, 1982): 26
7. Ibid.
8. "Creating a Creature," *Time* (May 31, 1982): 60
9. Todd McCarthy, "Sand Castles," *Film Comment* (May-June, 1982): 54-55

Chapter 8. THE COLOR OF LIFE
1. "I Dream for a Living," *Time* (July 15, 1985): 61
2. Ibid.
3. "The Wizard of Wonderland," *Newsweek* (June 4, 1984): 83A
4. Ibid., 79
5. Michael Sragow, "Will Hollywood's Mr. Perfect Ever Grow Up?" *Rolling Stone* (July 19/August 2, 1984): 32
6. "I Dream for a Living," *Time* (July 15, 1985): 61
7. "Whoopee for Whoopi," *Newsweek* (December 30, 1985): 60
8. Alice Walker, "In the Closet of the Soul," *Ms* (November, 1986): 32
9. "The Wizard of Wonderland," *Newsweek* (June 4, 1984): 80
10. Ibid., 83A

# Steven Spielberg 1947-

1947  Steven Spielberg is born in Cincinnati, Ohio, on December 18. *The Diary of Anne Frank* is published. Norwegian explorer Thor Heyerdahl sails on a raft from Peru to Polynesia to prove prehistoric migration. The Dead Sea Scrolls are discovered in Jordan. Bell Laboratories scientists invent the transistor. Jackie Robinson becomes the first black to sign a contract with a major league baseball club. More than one million American war veterans enroll in college under the G.I. Bill of Rights.

1948  John Huston's *The Treasure of Sierra Madre* is released. Mohandas Gandhi, of India, is assassinated. Chiang Kai-shek is reelected president of China. The State of Israel comes into existence. Harry Truman is elected president of the U.S.

1949  The Communist People's Republic of China is proclaimed with Mao Tse-tung in power. Israel is admitted to the United Nations. The U.S.S.R. tests its first atomic bomb.

1950  President Truman instructs the U.S. Atomic Energy Commission to develop the hydrogen bomb. Senator Joseph McCarthy charges that Communists have infiltrated the U.S. government. Antihistamines become a popular remedy for colds and allergies. There are 1.5 million TV sets in the U.S.

1951  Julius and Ethel Rosenberg are sentenced to death in the U.S. for espionage. Color TV is first introduced in the U.S.

1952  General Dwight D. Eisenhower is elected president. The first hydrogen bomb is exploded in the Pacific by the U.S. Queen Elizabeth comes to the British throne.

1953  Most U.S. movie theaters are adapted for CinemaScope film projection. Lung cancer is reported to be attributable to cigarette smoking. Edmund Hillary and Tenzing Norgay become the first to climb Mt. Everest.

1954  The U.S. Supreme Court rules that racial segregation in schools is a violation of the Fourteenth Amendment to the Constitution. Senator Joseph McCarthy continues his witch-hunting activities culminating in a nationally televised hearing to prove Communist infiltration into the U.S. army. Twenty-nine million U.S. homes have TV.

1955  The U.S. Air Force Academy opens, patterned after West Point and Annapolis. Blacks in Montgomery, Alabama, boycott segregated bus lines. Atomically generated electrical power is first used in Schenectady, New York. Commercial TV begins broadcasting in Britain.

1956  Rock-and-roll dancing comes into vogue. Soviet troops march into Hungary. Eisenhower is reelected president of the U.S. Transatlantic cable telephone service is inaugurated. Elvis Presley gains in popularity.

1957  Britain explodes thermonuclear bomb in the Pacific. Eisenhower formulates doctrine for protection of Middle Eastern nations from Communist aggression.

1958  Fidel Castro begins total war against the Batista government in Cuba. The European Common Market is founded. Tension grows in the U.S. as desegregation of schools is attempted in the South. Stereophonic recordings are developed in Britain.

1959  Castro becomes premier of Cuba. Alaska becomes the 49th U.S. state. Hawaii becomes the 50th state of the U.S. The first International Congress of Oceanography is held in New York.

1960  *Shoot the Piano Player*, directed by François Truffaut, is released. Richard Nixon and John F. Kennedy take part in first debates between presidential candidates on national television. Kennedy is elected president of the U.S. The first weather satellite transmits TV images of cloud cover all over the world. The U.S. has 85 million TV sets.

1961  Truffaut's *Jules and Jim* premieres. Cuban exiled rebels attempt an unsuccessful invasion of Cuba at the "Bay of Pigs." "Freedom Riders," white and black liberals, organized to test and force integration in the South, are attacked and beaten.

1962  Steven Spielberg, aged 15, directs *Firelight*, a film about aliens from outer space. Kennedy announces establishment of Russian missile base in Cuba and sets up blockade, but then withdraws it when Russia agrees to dismantle missiles.

1963  The Spielberg family moves to California. Riots and beatings by white and police mark civil-rights demonstrations in Birmingham, Alabama. John F. Kennedy is assassinated and succeeded by Vice-President Lyndon B. Johnson. U.S. sends aid to antigovernment forces in South Vietnam.

1964 A major earthquake occurs in Alaska. U.S. involvement in Vietnam conflict escalates.

1965 Lyndon B. Johnson is inaugurated as president of the U.S. Violence breaks out in Selma, Alabama. Martin Luther King, Jr. leads procession of 4,000 civil-rights demonstrators from Selma to Montgomery.

1967 Steven Spielberg enters California State College at Long Beach. Spielberg meets George Lucas and sees the screening of Lucas's film *THX 1138:4EB.* Six-day War between Israel and the Arab nations begins. Jerusalem is proclaimed unified city under Israeli rule. Martin Luther King, Jr. leads march against Vietnam War.

1968 U.S. intelligence ship *Pueblo* is captured by North Korea. Martin Luther King, Jr. is assassinated. Senator Robert F. Kennedy assassinated. Riots and brutality mark the Democratic Convention in Chicago. Richard M. Nixon elected president of the U.S.

1969 Spielberg becomes director of TV series, *Night Gallery.* First U.S. troops withdrawn from Vietnam. Protests against the war escalate.

1970 Steven Spielberg's first film, *Amblin',* is released along with *Love Story.* Spielberg begins directing TV shows, *Marcus Welby* and *Name of the Game,* and a TV movie, *Something Evil.* Truffaut's *The Wild Child* opens. It is estimated that there are 231 million TV sets in use around the world.

1971 Spielberg's *Duel* is seen on TV. Eighteen year olds get the vote in the U.S. Cigarette ads are banned from U.S. television.

1972 Francis Ford Coppola's movie, *The Godfather,* is released. Nixon becomes president; he visits China and the U.S.S.R. About 78 million TV sets are operating in the U.S. Five men are caught outside the Democratic National Headquarters—the beginning of the Watergate affair. Nixon reelected president in a landslide. Strict antihijacking measures are instituted at U.S. airports. Arab terrorists kill two Israeli Olympic athletes in Munich, West Germany. The military draft is phased out as the U.S. army becomes volunteer.

1973 *Savage* premieres on TV. Spielberg writes the film *Sugarland Express,* his first American theatrical motion picture. Steven writes the screenplay, *Ace Eli and Rodger of the Skies,* which is eventually filmed by director John Erman. *The Sting* wins the Academy Award for best picture. The five original Watergate defendants plead guilty. War between Arabs and Israelis rages on. World oil shortage sets off energy crisis.

1974 *Duel* premieres in Europe. Nixon resigns after tapes of White House conversations in the Watergate affair damage him. Vice-President Gerald R. Ford becomes president. Frank Robinson becomes the first black to manage a baseball team.

1975 Spielberg's film *Jaws* is released. Communist forces overrun South Vietnam. U.S. ends two decades of involvement in the Vietnam War.

1976 U.S. and U.S.S.R. sign treaty limiting underground nuclear explosions. U.S. celebrated its bicentennial. North and South Vietnam are reunited. The Episcopal church approves the ordination of women as priests and bishops.

1977 *Close Encounters of the Third Kind* is a Spielberg triumph. *Star Wars,* directed by George Lucas, appears. President Jimmy Carter grants a pardon to almost all draft evaders of the Vietnam War. The TV dramatization of *Roots* is a big hit. Oil flows through the Alaska pipeline.

1978 Violence sweeps Nicaragua in nationwide leftist campaign to overthrow President Samoza. U.S. ratifies Panama Canal treaties. A test-tube baby is born in England. Thor Heyerdahl sails on a wood boat from Iraq to the coast of Djibouti. Menachem Begin of Israel and Anwar Sadat of Egypt sign the Camp David accords for peace in the Middle East.

1979 Spielberg produces *1941.* A major accident occurs at a nuclear reactor on Three Mile Island, Pennsylvania. Some 90 people, including 63 Americans, are taken hostage at the American Embassy in Teheran, Iran, by militant followers of the Ayatollah Khomeini, who demanded the return of the Shah from the U.S.

1980 Spielberg produces *Used Cars.* Eight Americans are killed and 5 wounded in an ill-fated attempt to rescue the American hostages in Teheran. Ronald Reagan is elected president of the U.S. Former Beatle John Lennon is shot in Central Park, New York.

1981 *Raiders of the Lost Ark* swamps the box office. Moments after the inauguration of President Reagan, 52 American hostages in Iran are flown to safety in return for $8 billion in frozen assets to Iran. Sandra Day O'Connor becomes the first woman justice of the Supreme Court.

1982 *Poltergeist* and *E.T.: The Extra-Terrestrial* are released with great praise for Spielberg.

1984 *Gremlins* and *Indiana Jones and the Temple of Doom* are produced by Spielberg. Nicaragua accuses the U.S. of aiding the contras and mining its ports. Reagan and Vice-President George Bush are renominated to run against Walter Mondale and Geraldine Ferraro, the first woman to run for vice-president of the U.S. Indira Gandhi, prime minister of India, is slain by her own bodyguards. Reagan and Bush are reelected.

1985 *The Goonies*, a TV series, *Young Sherlock Holmes*, and *Back to the Future*, as well as *The Color Purple*, are Spielberg projects this year. Steven and Amy Irving are wed and their son, Max, is born. U.S. House of Representatives rejects request from President Reagan for military aid to the Nicaragua contras, but votes to provide $27 million in humanitarian aid. Public concern grows about a fatal disease called AIDS, Acquired Immune Deficiency Syndrome.

1986 Spielberg's *The Money Pit* is released. Mikhail Gorbachev, 54 years old, succeeds Chernenko as leader of the U.S.S.R.

1987 Spielberg releases *Innerspace* and *Empire of the Sun*. President Oscar Arias of Costa Rica proposed a peace plan for Central America; receives the Nobel Prize for peace. Reagan and Gorbachev sign a historic arms-limitation treaty.

1988 Spielberg produces *Who Framed Roger Rabbit* and *The Land Before Time*. Home videos of *E.T.* sell 15 million units. The Walt Disney Company produces *Oliver & Company*. George Lucas produces *Willow*. George Bush is elected U.S. President. The USSR introduces some capitalistic measures into the Soviet economy and cuts military spending. The Arab-Israeli conflict appears to wind down, and there is a cease-fire in the Iran-Iraq war.

1989 *Indiana Jones and the Last Crusade* (the third and last in the series of Indiana Jones' adventures), produced by George Lucas and directed by Steven Spielberg, is released, setting new records for ticket sales, grossing over $100 million in less than 20 days. The "Greenhouse Effect," ozone depletion, acid rain and radiation contamination become American environmental concerns. An Iran-Iraq truce is reached.

1990-1991 "Tiny Toon Adventures," depicting new animated characters related to Bugs Bunny and other cartoon figures and stressing their interactions with the adult cartoon figures, is produced by Warner Bros. with Spielberg acting as Executive Producer, fulfilling one of his passions for animation. Spielberg's version of "Peter Pan" called *Hook*, starring Julia Roberts, Robin Williams, Dustin Hoffman, and Maggie Smith is released in late 1991. Communist rule falls in Russia as wars break out in individual states seeking independence from the Soviet Union. East and West Germany are reunited after a 45-year division. A severe earthquake hits Northern California. Black nationalist leader Nelson Mandela is released from prison in South Africa. Iraq overruns Kuwait with the U.S. and other nations sending military forces that finally prevail. The Food and Drug Administration approves use of a drug for AIDS cases as the epidemic reaches its peak in the U.S.

1992-1993 *Jurassic Park*, the science-fiction thriller about a theme park populated by genetically engineered prehistoric beasts, with the dinosaurs being animated by specially developed computer programs, is directed by Spielberg; he reaches an agreement with the World Jewish Congress allowing him to build a replica of the Nazi death camp at Ocwiecim (Auschwitz), Poland, outside its main gates for the location of his future movie *Schindler's List*. As the Soviet Union dissolves and the Commonwealth of Independent States evolves, the Russian Federation makes radical economic reforms eliminating state subsidies on most goods and services causing prices to soar beyond the means of ordinary workers along with complex economic problems; in California two rare condors, in captivity for breeding, are released into the wild to begin restoring the birds to their natural habitat; delegates from 178 countries attended a United Nations Earth Summit and approve actions to prevent further environmental destruction; Israel and the Palestine Liberation Organization (PLO) reach peace terms.

# INDEX- *Page numbers in boldface type indicate illustrations.*

# About the Author

Jim Hargrove has worked as a writer and editor for more than ten years. After serving as an editorial director for three Chicago area publishers, he began a career as an independent writer, preparing a series of books for children. He has contributed to works by nearly twenty different publishers. His Childrens Press titles include biographies of Mark Twain, Daniel Boone, Thomas Jefferson, Lyndon B. Johnson, and Richard Nixon. With his wife and daughter, he lives in a small Illinois town near the Wisconsin border.